Benchmark Assessments

Grade 2

Benchmark
Assessments

www.mheonline.com/readingwonders

Mc
Graw
Hill
Education

Send all inquiries to:
McGraw-Hill Education
Two Penn Plaza
New York, New York 10121

ISBN: 978-0-07-679861-2
MHID: 0-07-679861-5

Printed in the United States of America.

2 3 4 5 6 7 QVS 20 19 18 17 16
B

Table of Contents

Teacher Introduction iv

Benchmark Test 1

    Session 1 1

    Session 2 21

Benchmark Test 2

    Session 1 39

    Session 2 58

Benchmark Test 3

    Narrative Performance Task 78

    Informational Performance Task 85

    Opinion Performance Task 93

    Answer Keys 101

Teacher Introduction

Benchmark Assessments

Benchmark Assessments is an integral part of the complete assessment program aligned with *Reading Wonders,* state standards, and advances in summative assessment that feature performance-based tasks, such as the Smarter Balanced Assessment Consortium (SBAC) assessment system.

Purpose of *Benchmark Assessments*

Benchmark Assessments reports on the outcome of student learning and provides summative data in relation to progress through the curriculum. The results of the assessments can be used to inform subsequent instruction, aid in making leveling and grouping decisions, and point toward areas in need of reteaching or remediation. The tests in *Benchmark Assessments* are constructed to mirror the approach and subject concentration found in state-mandated end-of-year and performance-based assessments, such as the SBAC End of Year (EOY) English Language Arts (ELA) test and SBAC performance-based assessments. Although students will not take part in SBAC testing this year, performance in these assessments can act as a signal of student readiness for the demands of high-stakes testing as well as a snapshot of student progress toward end-of-year goals.

Focus of *Benchmark Assessments*

The tests focus on the following key areas of ELA:

- Comprehension of literature and informational text
- Using text features to access or clarify information
- Vocabulary acquisition and use
- Research skills
- Drafting, editing, and revising text
- Command of the conventions of standard English language
- Writing to sources within the parameters of specific genres

Assessment Items Featured in *Benchmark Assessments*

Benchmark assessments feature the following item types—selected response (SR), multiple selected response (MSR), evidence-based selected response (EBSR), constructed response (CR), technology-enhanced items (TE), and Performance Tasks (PT). (Please note that the print versions of TE items are available in this component; the full functionality of the items is available only through the online assessment.) This variety of item types provides multiple methods of assessing student understanding, allows for deeper investigation into skills and strategies, and provides students an opportunity to become familiar with the kinds of items and approaches they will encounter in high-stakes assessments.

Teacher Introduction

Overview of *Benchmark Assessments*

The *Benchmark Assessments* component consists of three tests—Benchmark Test 1, Benchmark Test 2, and Benchmark Test 3.

Test 1 focuses on key skills that are part of the instruction in Units 1-3, Test 2 samples key skills from Units 1-6, and Test 3 features a suite of PTs.

Test 1 and Test 2 feature **39** items that mirror the focus and presentation students will encounter in end-of-year testing. The tests are broken into two sessions. A listening comprehension section has been omitted from the print component so as to allow for ease of administration. One online version of Test 2 contains a listening comprehension section that can be administered, if you feel students will benefit from the experience.

Test 3 contains examples of PTs that are part of traditional performance-based assessment.

- Narrative
  - Students craft a narrative using information from the sources.
- Informational
  - Students write an article based on the sources and use information from the sources.
- Opinion
  - Students analyze the ideas in sources and state an opinion that they support using the sources.

Each PT assesses standards that address comprehension, research skills, genre writing, and the use of standard English language conventions (ELC). The stimulus texts and research questions in each task build toward the goal of the final writing topic.

Administering *Benchmark Assessments*

Benchmark Test 1 should be given to students after Unit 3 is complete. Benchmark 2 should be given to students close to the end of the year. The PTs in Test 3 can be administered at various times during the year. The Narrative Task can be given at the start of the year and again closer to the performance-based assessment date to measure student growth.

Due to the length of the test (and to provide students a test-taking experience that is in concert with standardized testing), the schedule below is suggested. (Session 1 and Session 2 can be spaced over two days or grouped together with a short break in between.)

- Session 1 of Tests 1 and 2—45 to 60 minutes
- Session 2 of Tests 1 and 2—35 to 50 minutes
- PTs in Test 3—90 to 100 minutes. (Provide students 30 to 40 minutes to read the stimulus materials and answer the research questions, and 60 to 70 minutes for planning, writing, and editing their responses. If desired, provide students a short break between these activities.)

Teacher Introduction

Scoring *Benchmark Assessments*

Items 1–39 in Tests 1 and 2 are each worth two points, for a 78-point assessment. Each part of an EBSR is worth 1 point; MSR and TE items should be answered correctly in full, though you may choose to provide partial credit. For written responses, use the correct response parameters provided in the Answer Key and the scoring rubrics listed below to assign a score.

Short Response Score: 2

The response is well-crafted and concise and shows a thorough understanding of the underlying skill. Appropriate text evidence is used to answer the question.

Short Response Score: 1

The response shows partial understanding of the underlying skill. Text evidence is featured, though examples are too general.

Each PT is a 15-point assessment. For PT full-writes, use the rubrics on the following pages. Score the task holistically on a 10-point scale: 4 points for purpose/organization [P/O]; 4 points for evidence/elaboration [E/E] or development/elaboration [D/E]; and 2 points for English language conventions [C].

Evaluating Scores

The goal of each test is to evaluate student mastery of previously-taught material and to gauge preparedness for state-mandated testing.

Test 1 can serve as a summative, mid-year assessment.

Test 2 can serve as a summative, EOY assessment.

The PTs that comprise Test 3 can be assigned at points directly following specific instruction in the task genre to assess student mastery.

The expectation is for students

- to score 80% or higher on Tests 1 and 2; and

- to score "12" or higher on each PT.

For students who do not meet these benchmarks, assign appropriate lessons from the Tier 2 online PDFs. Use student results in particular test categories to guide intervention.

Use the rubrics to score the task holistically on a 10-point scale:
4 points for purpose/organization [P/O]; 4 points for evidence/elaboration [E/E] or development/elaboration [D/E]; and 2 points for English language conventions [C]

Unscorable or **Zero** responses are unrelated to the topic, illegible, contain little or no writing, or show little to no command of the conventions of standard English.

Teacher Introduction

Teacher Introduction

INFORMATIVE PERFORMANCE TASK SCORING RUBRIC

Score	Purpose/Organization	Evidence/Elaboration	Conventions
4	• **effective** organizational structure • clear statement of main idea based on purpose, audience, task • consistent use of various transitions • logical progression of ideas	• **convincing** support for main idea; **effective** use of sources • integrates comprehensive evidence from sources • relevant references • effective use of elaboration • audience-appropriate domain-specific vocabulary	
3	• **evident** organizational structure • adequate statement of main idea based on purpose, audience, task • adequate, somewhat varied use of transitions • adequate progression of ideas	• **adequate** support for main idea; **adequate** use of sources • some integration of evidence from sources • references may be general • adequate use of some elaboration • generally audience-appropriate domain-specific vocabulary	
2	• **inconsistent** organizational structure • unclear or somewhat unfocused main idea • inconsistent use of transitions with little variety • formulaic or uneven progression of ideas	• **uneven** support for main idea; **limited** use of sources • weakly integrated, vague, or imprecise evidence from sources • references are vague or absent • weak or uneven elaboration • uneven domain-specific vocabulary	• **adequate** command of spelling, capitalization, punctuation, grammar, and usage • few errors
1	• **little or no** organizational structure • few or no transitions • frequent extraneous ideas; may be formulaic • may lack introduction and/or conclusion • confusing or ambiguous focus; may be very brief	• **minimal** support for main idea; **little or no** use of sources • minimal, absent, incorrect, or irrelevant evidence from sources • references are absent or incorrect • minimal, if any, elaboration • limited or ineffective domain-specific vocabulary	• **partial** command of spelling, capitalization, punctuation, grammar, and usage • some patterns of errors

Teacher Introduction

NARRATIVE PERFORMANCE TASK SCORING RUBRIC

Score	Purpose/Organization	Development/Elaboration	Conventions
4	• **fully sustained** organization; **clear focus** • effective, unified plot • effective development of setting, characters, point of view • transitions clarify relationships between and among ideas • logical sequence of events • effective opening and closing	• **effective** elaboration with details, dialogue, description • clear expression of experiences and events • effective use of relevant source material • effective use of various narrative techniques • effective use of sensory, concrete, and figurative language	
3	• **adequately sustained** organization; **generally maintained** focus • evident plot with loose connections • adequate development of setting, characters, point of view • adequate use of transitional strategies • adequate sequence of events • adequate opening and closing	• **adequate** elaboration with details, dialogue, description • adequate expression of experiences and events • adequate use of source material • adequate use of various narrative techniques • adequate use of sensory, concrete, and figurative language	
2	• **somewhat sustained** organization; **uneven focus** • inconsistent plot with evident flaws • uneven development of setting, characters, point of view • uneven use of transitional strategies, with little variety • weak or uneven sequence of events • weak opening and closing	• **uneven** elaboration with **partial** details, dialogue, description • uneven expression of experiences and events • vague, abrupt, or imprecise use of source material • uneven, inconsistent use of narrative technique • partial or weak use of sensory, concrete, and figurative language	• **adequate** command of spelling, capitalization, punctuation, grammar, and usage • few errors
1	• **basic** organization; **little or no** focus • little or no discernible plot; may just be a series of events • brief or no development of setting, characters, point of view • few or no transitional strategies • little or no organization of event sequence; extraneous ideas • no opening and/or closing	• **minimal** elaboration with **few or no** details, dialogue, description • confusing expression of experiences and events • little or no use of source material • minimal or incorrect use of narrative techniques • little or no use of sensory, concrete, and figurative language	• **partial** command of spelling, capitalization, punctuation, grammar, and usage • some patterns of errors

Teacher Introduction

OPINION PERFORMANCE TASK SCORING RUBRIC

Score	Purpose/Organization	Evidence/Elaboration	Conventions
4	• **effective** organizational structure; **sustained** focus • consistent use of various transitions • logical progression of ideas • effective introduction and conclusion • clearly communicated opinion for purpose, audience, task	• **convincing** support/evidence for main idea; **effective** use of sources; **precise** language • comprehensive evidence from sources is integrated • relevant, specific references • effective elaborative techniques • appropriate domain-specific vocabulary for audience, purpose	
3	• **evident** organizational structure; **adequate** focus • adequate use of transitions • adequate progression of ideas • adequate introduction and conclusion • clear opinion, mostly maintained, though loosely • adequate opinion for purpose, audience, task	• **adequate** support/evidence for main idea; **adequate** use of sources; **general** language • some evidence from sources is integrated • general, imprecise references • adequate elaboration • generally appropriate domain-specific vocabulary for audience, purpose	
2	• **inconsistent** organizational structure; **somewhat sustained** focus • inconsistent use of transitions • uneven progression of ideas • introduction or conclusion, if present, may be weak • somewhat unclear or unfocused opinion	• **uneven** support for main idea; **partial** use of sources; **simple** language • evidence from sources is weakly integrated, vague, or imprecise • vague, unclear references • weak or uneven elaboration • uneven or somewhat ineffective use of domain-specific vocabulary for audience, purpose	• **adequate** command of spelling, capitalization, punctuation, grammar, and usage • few errors
1	• **little or no** organizational structure or focus • few or no transitions • frequent extraneous ideas are evident; may be formulaic • introduction and/or conclusion may be missing • confusing opinion	• **minimal** support for main idea; **little or no** use of sources; **vague** language • source material evidence is minimal, incorrect, or irrelevant • references absent or incorrect • minimal, if any, elaboration • limited or ineffective use of domain-specific vocabulary for audience, purpose	• **partial** command of spelling, capitalization, punctuation, grammar, and usage • some patterns of errors

Teacher Introduction

Answer Keys in *Benchmark Assessments*

The Answer Keys have been constructed to provide the information needed to aid understanding of student performance.

Correct answers, content focus, standards alignment, and complexity information are listed.

15	B, E	Main Idea and Key Details	RI.2.2	DOK 2
16	D	Context Clues	L.2.4a	DOK 2
17A	C	Main Idea and Key Details	RI.2.2	DOK 2
17B	B	Main Idea and Key Details/Text Evidence	RI.2.2/RI.2.1	DOK 2

Scoring tables show distinct categories to pinpoint possible areas of intervention or enrichment.

Comprehension: Selected Response 1A, 1B, 2A, 2B, 4, 6A, 6B, 7A, 7B, 8A, 8B, 10, 12, 13, 21A, 21B, 23A, 23B, 24A, 24B, 27, 28, 29A, 29B, 30A, 30B, 32, 33	/34	%
Comprehension: Constructed Response 5, 28	/4	%
Vocabulary 3A, 3B, 9A, 9B, 11, 22A, 22B, 25A, 25B, 26, 31A, 31B	/14	%
Research 14, 15, 16, 17	/8	%
Drafting, Editing, Revising 18, 19, 20, 37, 38, 39	/12	%
English Language Conventions 34, 35, 36	/6	%
Total Benchmark Assessment Score	/78	%

For PTs, SR items are worth 1 point each. CR items are worth 2 points each. Use the rubrics to score the full-write. An anchor paper response can be found for each PT. This top-line response is included to assist with scoring.

Narrative Performance Task				
Question	**Answer**	**CCSS**	**Complexity**	**Score**
1	B, D		DOK 3	/1
2	see below	RI.2.1, RI.2.2, RI.2.7, RI.2.8, RI.2.9 W.2.2, W.2.3a–e, W.2.4, W.2.7 L.2.1, L.2.2	DOK 3	/2
3	see below		DOK 3	/2
Story	see below		DOK 4	/4 [P/O] /4 [D/E] /2 [C]
Total Score				/15

SESSION 1

Read the passage. Then answer the questions.

Crow's Message

Crow perched on a tree branch in the town park. He looked down at the other animals. They were taking each other's food. They were poking each other. They were making fun of each other.

"What is the matter with you?" Crow scolded. "Why can't you be nice?" he shouted.

Crow gave a long speech. He told the animals how disgusting their behavior was. He even recited a poem:

You don't know how to act,
And that is a true fact!
You never show you care.
It's more than I can bear!

None of the animals even looked at Crow.

"I guess I have to try another way to get through to them," he thought. "I will try e-mail." So he typed a note to each of the animals. He commanded them to be polite. He ordered them to share. He ended with, "If you don't, you will be sorry!"

Not one animal mentioned the e-mail. The animals were still unkind and selfish.

"I need a more exciting way to deliver my message," Crow decided. He made a long banner. He picked up one end in his beak. Then he flew back and forth above the park. He tried to get the animals' attention. The animals continued their activities and paid no attention to the sign.

GO ON →

Down on the ground, Rabbit was hopping around the base of a tree looking for tender green leaves to eat. He saw a pile of acorns. Rabbits are not fond of acorns, so he started to kick them out of his way. Then he thought, "Squirrels like acorns. I could tell Squirrel they are here." He waved to Squirrel, who thought Rabbit was probably trying to play a mean trick on him. But he was curious, so he ran over to Rabbit.

Squirrel was very pleased with the crunchy acorns. "Looking for food is a full-time job," said Squirrel. "It is nice to have some help. Thank you." Rabbit felt good about helping.

Squirrel dashed off toward the other side of the park. On the way, he saw Mouse. She was stretching high trying to reach some twigs to make a nest. Squirrel started to make fun of Mouse for being so little. Then he stopped. He reached up and grabbed a bunch of twigs. He gave them to Mouse.

"Thank you!" said Mouse with surprise.

Mouse felt very good, so she was friendly to Duck. Then Duck helped Cricket. Soon, all the animals were being kind and helpful. Crow watched in amazement from his perch. Owl flew up to keep him company.

Crow said, "You are smart, Owl. Help me understand what happened. I tried to get the animals to be kind. They paid no attention. Now, they are all being friendly to each other."

"The reason is easy," said Owl. "Actions speak louder than words. You tried to tell them what to do, but Rabbit showed them. Good deeds are like seeds. Once they are planted, they can grow."

GO ON →

Name: _____   Date: _____

1 Read the poem from the passage.

You don't know how to act,
And that is a true fact!
You never show you care.
It's more than I can <u>bear</u>!

Which sentence uses <u>bear</u> in the **same** way it is used in the sentence above?

(A) The bear roared and showed its sharp claws.

(B) Henry can't bear to see his sister cry.

(C) Those beams bear the weight of the roof.

(D) Our peach trees bear quite a lot of fruit.

2 The following question has two parts. First, answer part A. Then, answer part B.

Part A: What is the first problem that Crow faces in the passage?

(A) The animals do not like Crow.

(B) The animals sit on Crow's branch.

(C) The animals do not pay attention to Crow.

(D) The animals like to listen to Crow's poem.

Part B: Which sentence from the passage **best** helps you answer part A?

(A) Crow perched on a tree branch in the town park.

(B) They were making fun of each other.

(C) Crow gave a long speech.

(D) None of the animals even looked at Crow.

GO ON →

3 Read the sentence from the passage.

He <u>commanded</u> them to be polite.

What is the root word of <u>commanded</u>?

Ⓐ command

Ⓑ comma

Ⓒ mand

Ⓓ ed

4 What does each character do in the story? Draw a line from the character to the event.

Crow   helps Cricket

Owl   is friendly to Duck

Mouse   explains what happened

Duck   gives acorns to Squirrel

Rabbit   recites a poem

GO ON →

5 How do the characters change in the story? Use **two** details from the story in your answer.

_____

_____

_____

_____

_____

Read the passage. Then answer the questions.

Shh! Someone Is Asleep!

We sleep to stay well. We sleep to get energy to work and play. Animals do, too.

Cozy in a Tree

Some animals sleep a lot. Koalas sleep 20 hours a day. They move very slowly when they wake up. Koalas are not lazy. They have a reason to be sleepy and slow. Their main food is a certain kind of leaf. These leaves are hard to digest. It takes a lot of energy for the koala's body to digest the leaves. Koalas must rest a lot to get enough energy.

Koalas sleep and eat in the same place—high in a tree.

Koalas sleep in the day. They wake up at night. They look for food. It would be easy for enemies to catch these slow animals. They spend their days and nights in trees. This helps them to keep safe from other animals. A high branch is their cozy, safe bed.

GO ON →

A Long Winter's Nap

Brown bears also sleep a lot. They nap for four to six months a year. A bear digs a den in a hill. It uses its claws. Then the bear crawls into this den to sleep.

It is hard to find food in cold weather. So bears sleep through the winter. Their hearts slow down. A bear's heart beats 70 times a minute when it is awake. A sleeping bear's heart beats just 10 times a minute. This helps them use less energy. Bears eat very big meals before their winter nap. They do not need to hunt for food until spring.

Asleep in the Deep

Sea animals sleep, too. Some sleep as they float in the water. Others find a safe spot to sleep. They might slide down deep into the mud or sneak behind a rock so no one can see them.

African mudfish live in streams. The streams dry up in the summer. The mudfish must save itself from drying up, too. Its body gives off slime. The slime mixes with mud. The slime and mud form a sack like a sleeping bag around the fish. There is a little opening in the sack. There is a tube in the opening. The fish breathes through the tube. It sleeps until the stream flows again.

Dolphins sleep in the sea. They need a way to breathe as they nap. Their bodies hold a lot of air. The air helps them float. A dolphin floats near the surface of the water as it sleeps. Its tail moves a bit once in a while. This pushes the dolphin up. The animal takes a breath of air. Then it floats down to rest some more.

Many sea animals swim at night. They rest during the day. Most fish do not have eyelids. Their eyes are wide open night and day.

GO ON →

A Wink of Sleep

Some land birds sleep in trees or barns. Others sleep in grasses. Most water birds sleep in shallow water. Others sleep on small pieces of land in the water. Some birds that live in cold places dig holes in snow. These holes are their beds.

Birds can sleep with one eye open and one shut. They can also sleep with half their brain awake. These tricks help them stay safe. It is hard for an enemy to sneak up on them.

Hours of Sleep Each Day	
Animal	How much it sleeps
brown bat	20 hours
armadillo	18 hours
lion	13 hours
dog	11 hours
horse	3 hours
giraffe	2 hours

Goodnight to All

Tonight, you will sleep in your bed. You will be safe and warm. Outside, lots of animals will be sleeping, too. They will be cozy in trees, holes, and streams.

GO ON →

6 The following question has two parts. First, answer part A. Then, answer part B.

Part A: What is the **most likely** reason the author chose to use pictures of a koala in a tree in the passage?

Ⓐ to show that koalas can see far if they are up high

Ⓑ to show that koalas spend most of their time in trees

Ⓒ to show that koalas climb trees faster than they can walk

Ⓓ to show that koalas are too tired to look for beds on the ground

Part B: Which sentence from the passage **best** helps you answer part A?

Ⓐ They move very slowly when they wake up.

Ⓑ It would be easy for enemies to catch these slow animals.

Ⓒ They spend their days and nights in trees.

Ⓓ A high branch is their cozy, safe bed.

7 The following question has two parts. First, answer part A. Then, answer part B.

Part A: Read the paragraphs from the passage.

Brown bears also sleep a lot. They nap for four to six months a year. A bear digs a den in a hill. It uses its claws. Then the bear crawls into this den to sleep.

It is hard to find food in cold weather. So bears sleep through the winter. Their hearts slow down. A bear's heart beats 70 times a minute when it is awake. A sleeping bear's heart beats just 10 times a minute. This helps them use less energy. Bears eat very big meals before their winter nap. They do not need to hunt for food until spring.

Why did the author **most likely** call this part of the passage "A Long Winter's Nap"?

Ⓐ Winters are very cold.

Ⓑ Bears hunt in the spring.

Ⓒ Many animals take naps.

Ⓓ Bears sleep for many months.

Part B: Which sentence from the passage **best** helps you answer part A?

Ⓐ Then the bear crawls into this den to sleep.

Ⓑ So bears sleep through the winter.

Ⓒ A sleeping bear's heart beats just 10 times a minute.

Ⓓ Bears eat very big meals before their winter nap.

GO ON →

8 The following question has two parts. First, answer part A. Then, answer part B.

Part A: Read the paragraph from the passage.

It is hard to find food in cold weather. So bears sleep through the winter. Their hearts slow down. A bear's heart beats 70 times a minute when it is awake. A sleeping bear's heart beats just 10 times a minute. This helps them use less energy. Bears eat very big meals before their winter nap. They do not need to hunt for food until spring.

Which sentence **best** describes the main idea of the paragraph?

(A) Bears do most of their hunting in the spring.

(B) When bears eat a lot, they need to take a nap.

(C) When bears are asleep, their hearts beat very slowly.

(D) Bears sleep all winter because they do not have much to eat.

Part B: Which sentence from the paragraph **best** helps you answer part A?

(A) It is hard to find food in cold weather.

(B) A sleeping bear's heart beats just 10 times a minute.

(C) Bears eat very big meals before their winter nap.

(D) They do not need to hunt for food until spring.

GO ON →

9 The following question has two parts. First, answer part A. Then, answer part B.

Part A: Read this sentence from the passage.

They might slide down deep into the mud or <u>sneak</u> behind a rock so no one can see them.

What does the word <u>sneak</u> **most likely** mean?

Ⓐ to move without being noticed

Ⓑ to move in a smooth way

Ⓒ to move around something

Ⓓ to move very quickly

Part B: Which words from the sentence **best** help you answer part A?

Ⓐ slide down deep

Ⓑ into the mud

Ⓒ behind a rock

Ⓓ no one can see them

GO ON →

10 The following question has two parts. First, answer part A. Then, answer part B.

Part A: Look at the chart near the end of the passage.

What is the **most likely** reason the author added the chart to the passage?

(A) to show that animals sleep for different amounts of time

(B) to show that some animals sleep more than people do

(C) to show that some animals do not need very much sleep

(D) to show that all animals need to get some sleep each day

Part B: Which sentence from the passage **best** helps you answer part A?

(A) We sleep to stay well.

(B) Some animals sleep a lot.

(C) Many sea animals swim at night.

(D) Tonight, you will sleep in your bed.

GO ON →

11 Which sentences from the passage **best** tell the main idea of the passage? Pick **three** choices.

Ⓐ We sleep to stay well.

Ⓑ Some animals sleep a lot.

Ⓒ Koalas sleep in the day.

Ⓓ Many sea animals swim at night.

Ⓔ Outside, lots of animals will be sleeping, too.

Ⓕ They will be cozy in trees, holes, and streams.

12 Which **one** of the following words from the passage is a compound word?

Ⓐ animals

Ⓑ energy

Ⓒ weather

Ⓓ eyelids

13 Why did the author **most likely** write this passage?

Ⓐ to teach about how different animals sleep

Ⓑ to tell the reader about the habits of koalas

Ⓒ to point out that ocean animals swim while they sleep

Ⓓ to show the reader that people need rest to get energy

Read the directions. Then answer the questions.

14 A student is writing a report about peacocks. She wrote an opinion in the report. Read the sentences from the student's report and the directions that follow.

My family took a trip to the zoo. We saw lots of different animals while we were there. The male peacock was my favorite. I love to watch it fan out its feathers. I think it is the most beautiful animal that there is.

The student found a source about peacocks. Choose **two** sentences from the source that **best** support the student's opinion.

Ⓐ A peacock can weigh up to 13 pounds.

Ⓑ Peacocks cannot fly like most other birds.

Ⓒ Peacock tail feathers shimmer in the light.

Ⓓ Some people keep blue peacocks as pets.

Ⓔ Peacocks have over 200 brightly colored feathers.

Ⓕ The natural habitat for peacocks is in forests and rainforests.

GO ON →

Name: _____ Date: _____

15 A student is writing a report about butterflies. The student took notes and thought of three main ideas for his report.

What main idea does each note support? Draw a line from the note to the main idea.

Butterflies can suck nectar from flowers.

How Big Do Butterflies Grow

Butterflies have four wings.

What Butterflies Look Like

Queen Alexandra's Birdwing is the largest butterfly.

What Butterflies Eat

Tiny scales on butterflies make them colorful.

16 A student is writing a report about insects. Which source would **most likely** have information for the report?

Ⓐ "Spiderman" comic book

Ⓑ "The Itsy Bitsy Spider" song

Ⓒ "The Life of a Spider" website

Ⓓ "Miss Spider's Tea Party" children's book

17 A student is writing a report about types of flowers. Which website is **most likely** to be a useful source of information for the report?

Ⓐ www.flowercrafts.net

Ⓑ www.marysflowerblog.com

Ⓒ www.dangerousflowers.gov

Ⓓ www.flowersoftheworld.edu

18 A student is writing an opinion letter to the principal about allowing frozen yogurt sales at school. Read the draft of the letter. Then complete the task that follows.

Dear Mr. Smith:

I want to ask that you sell frozen yogurt at school. You can sell it every day. Having frozen yogurt is better than having ice cream. It is healthier. Students can eat it at lunch for dessert. We can still have ice cream. Or, we can pick frozen yogurt for dessert. Students can pick flavors like vanilla or chocolate. Ice cream has a lot of sugar.

Sincerely, Jenny Wells

Write a paragraph that completes the letter supporting an opinion about selling frozen yogurt at school.

_____

_____

_____

_____

_____

19 A student is writing a report for science class about snakes. The student wants to **revise** the draft to delete details that do not support the main idea. Read the draft of the report. Then complete the task that follows.

Snakes are interesting animals. Snakes do not have noses. So, they use their forked tongues to smell. Some snakes, like a rattlesnake, cannot see very well. They use pit holes, which are openings in front of their eyes, to help them sense body heat. Snakes do not have ears. Instead, they have a bone in their lower jaw to help them feel movement. Some people do not like snakes. They have two fangs. Many snakes have venom, or poison, in their fangs. Snakes shed their skin. Their new skin looks shiny and wet.

Which sentence is the **best** way to revise the information in the underlined sentence?

Ⓐ Snakes can be weird.

Ⓑ Snakes can be nasty.

Ⓒ Snakes can be boring.

Ⓓ Snakes can be dangerous.

20 A student is writing a story for her class about playing outside. The student wants to **revise** the draft to introduce a character. Read the draft of the story. Then answer the question that follows.

"I wonder what I will do first?" she asked. First, Maddy decided to jump rope. "1, 2, 3, 4, 5!" Maddy sang. She loved to jump rope. No one was there to clap for her. Next, she wanted to play on the swings. "Whee!" Maddy shouted. But no one was there to push her or see how high she could go. She could almost reach the sky! Finally, she decided to join her friend Luke. "You know, Luke," Maddy said, "playing alone can be fun, but playing with a friend is even better!"

Choose the **best** beginning sentence to introduce the character.

- (A) Maddy wanted to play alone.
- (B) Maddy stumbled over a rock.
- (C) Maddy listened to the birds chirping.
- (D) Maddy smiled about playing with her friend.

SESSION 2

Read the passage. Then answer the questions.

Vet for a Day

Jack answered the phone. "Hi, Aunt Becky," he said.

"We are having a Bring a Child to Work Day where I work," Aunt Becky said cheerfully. "I want you to come so you can learn about my job."

Jack felt worried. Aunt Becky was a vet. She worked at an animal hospital. Jack thought it would be sad to see sick and injured animals. But he did not want to hurt Aunt Becky's feelings, so he agreed.

On the day of the visit, Aunt Becky picked up Jack very early. Jack did not look happy. "Don't worry," she said. "You will see all the good things that a vet does." She smiled at Jack. "First, I must check the sick animals that came in during the night to see if they are okay."

Jack saw how gentle and calm Aunt Becky was with her patients. The animals were happy to see Aunt Becky. The dogs wagged their tails and the cats purred. The birds chirped.

"How do you know what is wrong with them?" Jack asked. "They can't tell you like people can."

"I have to look very closely at each animal. I have to watch how they behave," she said. "This big cat is limping, so her leg must be hurt."

Next, it was time for surgery. "Oh no," thought Jack. "There could be blood. My tummy feels bad." But he did not have time to think about it. Aunt Becky gave him special clothes to put on. She took him into the surgery room.

GO ON →

Jack looked at the tiny dog on the table. Then he looked down at the floor. He did not want to see Aunt Becky operate on the dog. After a while, he got braver and took little peeks. Then he started watching the operation. Jack was amazed that Aunt Becky could work on such a small animal. Before he knew it, she was done.

"Will the dog be okay?" he asked.

"Yes, he just had a little bump on his belly. I had to take it off. Soon, he will be running around and feeling fine."

Next, Aunt Becky checked her list of animals to see for the day. The first was a kitten.

"He looks healthy," said Aunt Becky. "I will give him a shot to help him stay well."

"Uh-oh," thought Jack. "I don't like to get shots, and I'll bet the kitten will cry." But Jack was surprised. Aunt Becky touched the kitten gently. She talked to him softly as she gave him the shot. The kitten did not seem to mind the shot.

GO ON →

Aunt Becky spent the rest of the morning seeing cats, dogs, birds, and even a rabbit. Sometimes, the animals just needed a checkup. Sometimes, they were sick. Aunt Becky always knew what to do.

Jack was hungry. "When is lunch?" he asked.

"Who has time for lunch?" Aunt Becky teased. "We have to eat while we work." Jack sat in a wooden armchair in her office and munched on a sandwich. Aunt Becky ate at her desk and wrote notes about the animals she saw in the morning.

There were more patients after lunch. Jack was tired by the end of the day. At last, Aunt Becky dropped him off at home. She said, "That wasn't so bad, was it?" She winked at Jack. Jack smiled at Aunt Becky. "I was wrong. Being a vet isn't sad at all," he said. "Maybe I will be a vet when I grow up. It feels good to help animals!"

GO ON →

21 The following question has two parts. First, answer part A. Then, answer part B.

Part A: What is Jack's main problem at the beginning of the passage?

(A) He wants to learn about a different job.

(B) He does not like to spend time with Aunt Becky.

(C) He knows how to take care of sick animals.

(D) He does not want to go to the animal hospital.

Part B: Which sentence from the passage **best** supports your answer in part A?

(A) "I want you to come so you can learn about my job."

(B) Jack thought it would be sad to see sick and injured animals.

(C) On the day of the visit, Aunt Becky picked up Jack very early.

(D) "You will see all the good things that a vet does."

GO ON →

22 The following question has two parts. First, answer part A. Then, answer part B.

Part A: How does Aunt Becky check the animals that came to the hospital during the night?

   Ⓐ She calls Jack on the telephone.

   Ⓑ She looks closely at each animal.

   Ⓒ She operates on a tiny dog.

   Ⓓ She writes notes about the animals.

Part B: Which sentence from the passage **best** supports your answer in part A?

   Ⓐ "You will see all the good things that a vet does."

   Ⓑ "How do you know what is wrong with them?" Jack asked.

   Ⓒ "This big cat is limping, so her leg must be hurt."

   Ⓓ "He looks healthy," said Aunt Becky.

23 The following question has two parts. First, answer part A. Then, answer part B.

Part A: How does Jack change from the beginning to the end of the passage?

(A) First Jack feels sick, but later he feels better.

(B) First Jack feels happy, but later he feels tired.

(C) First Jack feels worried, but later he feels excited.

(D) First Jack feels hungry, but later he feels sorry.

Part B: Which sentence from the passage **best** helps you answer part A?

(A) "My tummy feels bad."

(B) "We have to eat while we work."

(C) "That wasn't so bad, was it?"

(D) "It feels good to help animals!"

24 Put the events from the passage in the correct order. Write 1, 2, 3, or 4 on the line next to each event.

_____ Jack looked at the tiny dog on the table.

_____ Before he knew it, she was done.

_____ Aunt Becky gave him special clothes to put on.

_____ She took him into the surgery room.

25 Which words from the passage are compound words? Make **two** choices.

Ⓐ cheerfully

Ⓑ hospital

Ⓒ operation

Ⓓ sometimes

Ⓔ armchair

26 Which sentence from the passage **best** shows that Aunt Becky was very busy at the animal hospital?

Ⓐ Jack saw how gentle and calm Aunt Becky was with her patients.

Ⓑ The animals were happy to see Aunt Becky.

Ⓒ Next, Aunt Becky checked her list of animals to see for the day.

Ⓓ "Who has time for lunch?" Aunt Becky teased.

27 Read the sentence from the passage.

The kitten did not seem to <u>mind</u> the shot.

What does <u>mind</u> mean in the sentence?

(A) babysit

(B) care about

(C) understand

(D) listen to

28 How does Aunt Becky help Jack solve his problem? Support your answer with details from the story.

_____

_____

_____

_____

_____

Read the passage. Then answer the questions.

Nature's Light Shows

Lightning is one of nature's light shows. It is fun to watch, but it can also cause harm. You need to know the facts about lightning. The facts will help you be safe.

Giant Sparks

Flashes of lightning are huge sparks of electric power. The sparks let off a bright light. Lightning is very hot, too. It heats the air around it. The hot air moves very fast. This moving air makes a loud boom that is called thunder and can sound like an explosion.

Light moves faster than sound. First, we see the lightning. Then, we hear the thunder.

There are different kinds of lightning. Most lightning travels from cloud to cloud. Some lightning travels from clouds to the ground.

Cloud to cloud lightning goes across the sky.

Cloud to ground lightning goes from the sky down to earth.

GO ON →

Lightning can also travel from the ground to the clouds. But all kinds of lightning are sparks of electricity.

Inside, Not Outside

Lightning is beautiful. It is exciting. It can also cause harm. To be safe, stay inside during storms with lightning. Stay away from windows.

Do not use anything that is electric. Lightning can go through wires. Remind your parents to unplug things like TVs and computers. Some people who get hurt in their homes during a storm are using a phone with a cord. Cell phones are okay to use.

Do not take a shower when there is lightning. Do not wash your hands. Remind your parents not to use the washer. Lightning can go through water. Do something safe. You can read a book or play a board game.

Even after the rain stops, there can still be lightning. Do not rush outside as quickly as a bunny. Stay indoors for a while to be sure the storm is over.

Lightning can harm the earth, too. When lightning hits land, it can cause a fire. Many wildfires start because of summer lightning. The land is dry. Twigs and grasses are dry. They burn easily.

Lightning Lessons

Scientists study lightning. They learn facts about it. They use cameras. The cameras go into space on spacecrafts called satellites. The cameras take pictures of lightning strikes. Scientists make maps to show what they learn.

GO ON →

They have found out that Africa has more lightning than anywhere in the world. Parts of Africa get lightning all year round. Why is this? It is because lightning happens most often in hot, wet places. Florida has more lightning than anywhere in the United States. It is hot and wet there, too.

We know that lightning almost never happens at the North or South Pole. Also, there is not much lightning around islands in the Pacific Ocean.

Around the world, there are about 2,000 lightning storms happening this minute. There are about 100 lightning strikes every second.

Enjoy the Show!
Lightning is an exciting part of nature. Learn about it. Learn how to stay safe. Then you can enjoy nature's light shows.

GO ON →

29 The following question has two parts. First, answer part A. Then, answer part B.

Part A: What is the **most likely** reason the author used pictures of lightning in the passage?

(A) to show what causes lightning

(B) to show that lightning is dangerous

(C) to show different kinds of lightning

(D) to show the number of lightning strikes

Part B: Which pair of sentences from the passage **best** helps you answer part A?

(A) The sparks let off a bright light. Lightning is very hot, too.

(B) Most lightning travels from cloud to cloud. Some lightning travels from clouds to the ground.

(C) It can also cause harm. To be safe, stay inside during storms with lightning.

(D) Around the world, there are about 2,000 lightning storms happening this minute. There are about 100 lightning strikes every second.

GO ON →

30 The following question has two parts. First, answer part A. Then, answer part B.

Part A: Read the sentence from the passage.

This moving air makes a noisy boom that is called thunder and can sound like an <u>explosion</u>.

What does the word <u>explosion</u> **most likely** mean?

Ⓐ sizzling sound

Ⓑ fast change

Ⓒ loud noise

Ⓓ dangerous time

Part B: Which words from the sentence **best** help you answer part A?

Ⓐ This moving air

Ⓑ a noisy boom

Ⓒ is called thunder

Ⓓ can sound like

GO ON →

31 The following question has two parts. First, answer part A. Then, answer part B.

Part A: Read this sentence from the passage.

Do not rush outside <u>as quickly as a bunny</u>.

Why did the author use the <u>underlined</u> phrase in the sentence?

(A) to show that lightning moves fast like a bunny

(B) to show that animals need to be kept inside during storms

(C) to show that you should not go outside right after a storm

(D) to show that you should do something calm instead of running during storms

Part B: Which sentence from the passage **best** helps you answer part A?

(A) Light moves faster than sound.

(B) To be safe, stay inside during storms with lightning.

(C) You can read a book or play a board game.

(D) Stay indoors for a while to be sure the storm is over.

32 Which sentences from the passage **best** tell the main idea of the passage? Pick **two** choices.

(A) You need to know the facts about lightning.

(B) There are different kinds of lightning.

(C) Lightning is beautiful.

(D) Lightning can harm the earth, too.

(E) Scientists study lightning.

(F) Learn how to stay safe.

33 Which sentence from the passage **best** shows that the author wrote the passage to give information about lightning?

(A) The facts will help you be safe.

(B) Lightning is beautiful.

(C) You can read a book or play a board game.

(D) Lightning is an exciting part of nature.

Read the directions. Then answer the questions.

34 Which **two** sentences use the correct words for a group of animals?

Ⓐ A nest of ducks landed on the pond.

Ⓑ We ran quickly from the swarm of bees.

Ⓒ The herd of ants marched across the table.

Ⓓ The pack of wolves howled at the full moon.

Ⓔ A dog chased the flock of horses across the field.

Ⓕ A gang of fish swam by my foot as I stood in the water.

35 Choose the **two** sentences that have **no** errors using past-tense verbs.

Ⓐ I drinked all of the ice cold water.

Ⓑ When he left my house, I run after him.

Ⓒ My cat hid under the bed from the dog.

Ⓓ Yesterday, my mom and I drawed a picture together.

Ⓔ We drove several hours to get to the beach for vacation.

Ⓕ When I looked out of the window, I seen my cat climb a tree.

36 Which word correctly completes the sentence?

The five _____ swam slowly across the pond.

Ⓐ geese

Ⓑ goose

Ⓒ gooses

Ⓓ gice

GO ON →

37 A student is writing a story for his class about a family vacation. The student wants to make sure that he has words that are clear. Choose the phrase that **best** tells the student's meaning for the blank below.

After breakfast, my dad told my family to get set. We were going on a family vacation. It was going to be a lot of fun! We packed all of our things and jumped in the car to leave. We drove _____. We arrived at the beach around noon. We played in the sand and in the water. We built castles and filled buckets. We had a great time!

Ⓐ all morning long

Ⓑ in the dark

Ⓒ in the rain

Ⓓ forever and ever

38 A student is writing a report about a book she read. Read the draft of the report. Then answer the question.

The story takes place a long time ago. A **dude** and his family are moving from England to the United States. They have many troubles along the way. The baby gets sick. The ship gets caught in a storm. They finally get to the U.S. and find a home.

The student has decided that the **bold** word is not the best word to use in the report. Which word is the **best** choice to replace the bold word?

Ⓐ men   Ⓒ man

Ⓑ human   Ⓓ person

GO ON →

39 A student is writing a story for her teacher about catching a bug. Read the draft of the story. Then answer the question that follows.

My brother and I caught a bug. My mom is scared of bugs. We put the bug in a jar and took it to show her. She looked in the jar. She was <u>shaking in her boots</u>. My brother and I let the bug go in the yard.

What is the best way to say what the writer means by the underlined phrase?

Ⓐ really angry

Ⓑ very scared

Ⓒ running fast

Ⓓ laughing hard

Grade 2 • Benchmark Assessment • Test 1

SESSION 1

Read the passage. Then answer the questions.

A Very Special Celebration

"I have a surprise for you," Mr. Black told his class. "The Thanksgiving holiday is coming soon. We will have a class Thanksgiving party. Everyone can bring a special dish their family makes for Thanksgiving."

The children cheered and clapped. Mike said he would bring sliced turkey. Pam said she would ask her grandfather to make his pumpkin pie. Don promised to bring his mother's tasty stuffing. All the children were busy planning the party, except Lang. She was silent and did not share any ideas.

When Lang got home from school, she ran into the house looking for her mother. "What is the matter, Lang?" Mom asked. "You look unhappy."

"We are having a Thanksgiving party at school. I don't know what Thanksgiving is," said Lang.

"Of course you don't know. We only moved to the United States a few months ago. We haven't had an American Thanksgiving yet," Mom explained.

"Mr. Black said to bring Thanksgiving food. We don't know how to make Thanksgiving food," Lang said.

"Don't worry. We'll think of something to do," Mom promised her.

Mom told Lang, "Long ago, people from Europe came to the United States. Native Americans already lived here. They taught the new people how to farm the land. In the summer, the people gathered their crops. In the fall, the new people

GO ON →

and the Native Americans had a party. They were happy for the food they had grown. They celebrated their harvest."

"So Thanksgiving is like our Mid-Autumn Festival in Vietnam! They both celebrate the harvest. I could share some of our traditions at the party," said Lang. Mom smiled.

The next day, Lang could not wait to get to school. Mr. Black was excited about Lang's idea. He told the class, "We will mix together American and Vietnamese customs at our party. Lang will bring moon cakes. She will show us how to make lanterns. She will help us make paper masks."

Claudio raised his hand. "My family came from Puerto Rico when I was five. We had a special holiday in the fall. We celebrated the plantain harvest. I could bring some plantain dishes. They are like bananas. They are yummy!"

Then Kami told the class that his grandma had just come to live with them. "She is from India," Kami said. "She told me about the Indian harvest festival. They eat pongal. It is a sweet rice dish. She can make some for us."

On the day of the party, families came to school with their children. Everyone carried dishes of food. Lang brought in a huge tray of moon cakes. The children put up decorations. They shared materials for crafts. They taught each other games. They danced to music from many places.

At the end of the day, Mr. Black said, "I want to share a tradition. My family does something special on Thanksgiving. We take turns telling something we are thankful for. Who wants to start?"

Lang raised her hand. "I'm thankful for new friends in my new country."

GO ON →

1 The following question has two parts. First, answer part A. Then, answer part B.

Part A: Which sentence **best** tells what Lang learns in the passage?

(A) Thanksgiving is a celebration of harvest foods.

(B) Thanksgiving is best celebrated by eating a turkey.

(C) Thanksgiving can be a good time to make new friends.

(D) Thanksgiving can be celebrated in many different ways.

Part B: Which sentence from the passage **best** helps you answer part A?

(A) "Mr. Black said to bring Thanksgiving food."

(B) "They both celebrate the harvest."

(C) "We will mix together American and Vietnamese customs at our party."

(D) "I'm thankful for new friends in my new country."

2 Read the sentence from the passage.

She was <u>silent</u> and did not share any ideas.

What does the word <u>silent</u> **most likely** mean?

(A) angry

(B) quiet

(C) sad

(D) loud

GO ON →

3 The following question has two parts. First, answer part A. Then, answer part B.

Part A: Read the paragraph from the passage.

"So Thanksgiving is like our Mid-Autumn Festival in Vietnam! They both celebrate the harvest. I could share some of our traditions at the party," said Lang. Mom smiled.

Which sentence **best** states the main message of the paragraph?

(A) Thanksgiving is a celebration of the harvest.

(B) People in Vietnam also celebrate Thanksgiving.

(C) Thanksgiving is also called the Mid-Autumn Festival.

(D) Other countries have holidays that are like Thanksgiving.

Part B: Which sentence or phrase from the passage **best** helps you answer part A?

(A) "So Thanksgiving is like our Mid-Autumn Festival in Vietnam!"

(B) "They both celebrate the harvest."

(C) "I could share some of our traditions at the party."

(D) Mom smiled.

GO ON →

4 Choose the words that **best** complete the sentences about Lang and her mother.

When Lang tells her mother about the class party, Lang feels _____. After talking together, Lang and her mother _____.

Ⓐ angry, cannot decide what to bring

Ⓑ excited, work to find an answer

Ⓒ lazy, do not know what is needed for the party

Ⓓ sad, have different ideas about parties

5 What can the reader tell about Lang's feelings about the classroom Thanksgiving celebration at the end of the story? Use details from the story in your answer.

_____

_____

_____

_____

_____

GO ON →

Read the passage. Then answer the questions.

Do Not Smell These Flowers!

Smell the roses. Smell the lilac bush. But do not smell the flowers of the titan arum plant! They smell awful! These flowers smell like a dead animal or bad meat. People have nicknamed it the "corpse plant" because it smells like something that has died.

Corpse plants grow in the rainforest. Many live to be 40 years old. They grow quickly. They can grow as much as a few inches a day. Some grow to be 10 feet tall. The plant shoots out of a round bulb under the soil. This bulb is called a corm. Just this one part of the plant can weigh 200 pounds.

The size of these plants makes them unusual. But their smell is the real story. They do not make flowers until they are about 10 years old. First, the bud opens. That is when the awful smell begins. The bud is called the spathe. Inside the spathe is another part. It looks like a long stick. It is called the spadix. Flowers grow from the spadix. Then the flowers produce cherry-sized red fruits.

The corpse plant's odor makes you want to hold your nose. But some kinds of beetles and flies like it. They fly to the flower to smell more. It is important for insects to come to the plant. They get the plant's pollen on their feet. They carry it to other plants. This is what helps new plants to grow.

To make sure many insects come to it, the plant heats itself up. This helps the smell spread out, just as the smell of a scented candle does.

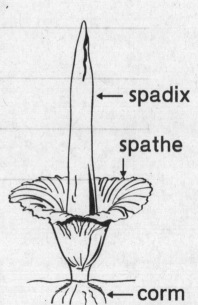

← spadix

spathe

← corm

GO ON →

It takes a lot of energy for the corpse plant to bloom and spread its smell. That is the reason the flowers only last for a day. It is also why the plants only bloom every two or three years. The plant goes through resting times and growing times. Every year, it makes one big leaf with a funny shape. The leaf looks like a giant green umbrella.

This plant does not grow in nature in the United States. But once in a blue moon, some scientists can grow it from seeds to learn more about it. The first corpse plant flower bloomed in this country at a public garden in New York in 1937. Since then, only about 100 corpse flowers have bloomed here.

One corpse plant at a public garden in California bloomed in 1999. It bloomed again in 2002 and 2009. A plant at a college in Illinois bloomed in 2011. A museum in Texas has two corpse plants. Visitors have named them Lois and Audrey.

The blooming of these plants is very special. People come to see how they look. They come to find out how bad the smell is. Scientists come to study them, too. For the first time, in 2011, a scientist collected some of the disgusting scent to study. His work may help us know more about this amazing plant.

6 The following question has two parts. First, answer part A. Then, answer part B.

Part A: How does the author connect ideas about the corpse plant in the passage?

(A) The author points out that the plant is very large, but its smell is what makes it really special.

(B) The author points out that the plant grows quickly, but its flowers are the most important thing about it.

(C) The author points out that the plant grows to be forty years old, but the weight of its bulb is the most unusual thing about it.

(D) The author points out that the plant's flowers do not last long, but the fact that scientists want to study it makes it really special.

Part B: Which sentence from the passage **best** helps you answer part A?

(A) Just this one part of the plant can weigh 200 pounds.

(B) But their smell is the real story.

(C) That is the reason the flowers only last for a day.

(D) But once in a blue moon, some scientists can grow it from seeds to learn more about it.

7 The following question has two parts. First, answer part A. Then, answer part B.

Part A: Read the sentence from the passage.

The size of these plants makes them unusual.

Which word **best** states the meaning of unusual?

(A) bad

(B) different

(C) exciting

(D) large

Part B: Which sentence from the passage **best** helps you answer part A?

(A) Just this one part of the plant can weigh 200 pounds.

(B) They smell awful!

(C) They do not make flowers until they are about 10 years old.

(D) Then the flowers produce cherry-sized red fruits.

8 Read the sentences from the passage.

This plant does not grow in nature in the United States. But <u>once in a blue moon</u>, some scientists can grow it from seeds to learn more about it.

What does the phrase "once in a blue moon" **most likely** mean?

(A) without a lot of trouble

(B) usually

(C) not very often

(D) not able to be done

9 The following question has two parts. First, answer part A. Then, answer part B.

Part A: What is the author's **main** purpose for writing about the corpse plant?

(A) to ask the reader to go see corpse plants

(B) to tell the reader how insects use corpse plants

(C) to give the reader information about corpse plants

(D) to entertain the reader with stories about corpse plants

Part B: Which sentence from the passage **best** helps you answer part A?

(A) Corpse plants grow in the rainforest.

(B) First, the bud opens.

(C) They fly to the flower to smell more.

(D) People come to see how they look.

GO ON →

10 The following question has two parts. First, answer part A. Then, answer part B.

Part A: Why did the author think that using pictures was important to understanding the corpse plant in the passage?

(A) The pictures give the reader an idea of where the corpse flower lives.

(B) The pictures give the reader an idea of what the corpse flower looks like.

(C) The pictures give the reader an idea of how bad the corpse flower smells.

(D) The pictures give the reader an idea of the people who study the corpse flower.

Part B: Which sentence from the passage **best** helps you answer part A?

(A) They smell awful!

(B) Corpse plants grow in the rainforest.

(C) Some grow to be 10 feet tall.

(D) Scientists come to study them, too.

GO ON →

11 Which sentences from the passage **best** tell an effect of the corpse plant using a lot of energy? Pick **two** choices.

(A) That is the reason the flowers only last for a day.

(B) It is also why the plants only bloom every two or three years.

(C) Every year, it makes one big leaf with a funny shape.

(D) The leaf looks like a giant green umbrella.

(E) Since then, only about 100 corpse flowers have bloomed here.

(F) The blooming of these plants is very special.

12 How do corpse plants use insects to help grow new plants? Write 1, 2, 3, 4, or 5 next to each step to show the correct order.

_____ The plant heats itself.

_____ Insects come to the plant.

_____ The plant's smell spreads.

_____ Insects carry pollen to other plants.

_____ Insects get pollen on their feet.

13 Read the paragraph from the passage. Then answer the question.

Corpse plants grow in the rainforest. Many live to be 40 years old. They grow quickly. They can grow as much as a few inches a day. Some grow to be 10 feet tall. The plant shoots out of a round bulb under the soil. This bulb is called a corm. Just this one part of the plant can weigh 200 pounds.

What is the main idea in this paragraph?

(A) Corpse plants are very large.

(B) Corpse plants grow daily.

(C) Corpse plants need rain.

(D) Corpse plants live a long time.

Read the directions. Then answer the questions.

14 A student is writing a report about reading. She found a source. Read **Source #1**. Then read the directions that follow.

Source #1

Reading by yourself is very important. Children get better grades when the teacher lets them read alone. Students are happier when they can choose their own reading books. Teachers do not have to teach new words. Students can learn new words when they read by themselves. That way, the teacher does not have so much work to do.

The student found a second source about reading. Choose **two** sentences from **Source #2** that support the author's opinion in **Source #1**.

Ⓐ Students can control what they choose to read.

Ⓑ Reading on their own helps students to remember better.

Ⓒ Students feel more comfortable when they can read by themselves.

Ⓓ Reading time for second graders should be about 20 minutes every day.

Ⓔ Schools with reading time for students have teachers who do more work.

Ⓕ Students learn less when they read on their own than students who do not.

GO ON →

15 A student is writing a report about gym class. He is looking for information about how long to exercise. Choose **two** sentences that have information about how long to exercise.

Ⓐ Gym class lasts for one hour.

Ⓑ Gym class lasts longer than recess.

Ⓒ Students can stay fit during gym class.

Ⓓ Students can go to recess for 15 minutes.

Ⓔ Students should exercise for about one hour.

Ⓕ Students should move around for 15 minutes at a time.

16 A student is writing a report about how to make a treehouse. Which website is **most likely** to be a useful source of information for her report?

Ⓐ www.welovetreehouses.com Read about how children love treehouses.

Ⓑ www.mytreehouseisfun.com Read about two friends who play in a treehouse.

Ⓒ www.treehouseplan.com Read about how to choose a tree for a treehouse.

Ⓓ www.costtobuildtreehouses.com Read about people who discuss the cost to build a treehouse.

17 A student is writing a report about frogs. Read the sentences from his report and the directions that follow.

The bumps on some frogs can be dangerous. The bumps contain poison. The poison can irritate the mouth of animals who might try to eat the frog. It is best to leave frogs alone.

Which source would **most likely** give the student more information about the ideas he has written?

(A) a website about the life cycle of frogs

(B) a journal entry about catching frogs

(C) a fact book about the features of different frogs

(D) a magazine article about saving frogs from other animals

18 A student is writing a story for his teacher about a boy who goes to a baseball game for the first time. Read the draft of the story and complete the task that follows.

Dale was excited. He was going to his first baseball game! His whole family was going. It was a beautiful, sunny day. The stadium was huge! First, the family got some snacks. Dale got a hot dog and soda. Then, the family found their seats. Soon, the game started. It was a close game!

Write one or two paragraphs that add description about what happens during and at the end of the game.

_____

_____

_____

_____

_____

_____

19 A student is writing an opinion letter for the school paper about morning recess. The student wants to revise the draft to improve the end of the letter. Read the draft of the letter. Then complete the task that follows.

Dear Miss Henry:

I think the second grade students should get a morning recess. We could go outside when the first graders do. We need to run around and get some exercise. It is good to be outside. It keeps our bodies healthy. It is almost four hours from when school starts to lunch recess. That is too long to sit still. If we get a morning recess, it will be a good break for our bodies. <u>We need a recess, so give one to us!</u>

Thank you,

Rowan Thornton

Choose the sentence that would **best** improve the ending, or <u>underlined</u> part, of the letter.

(A) A good principal would give us a morning recess.

(B) The teachers want us to have a morning recess, too.

(C) It is not fair that the first graders get a morning recess.

(D) A morning recess will help us work harder all day in school.

GO ON →

Name: _____ Date: _____

20 A student is writing a report for her teacher about good habits. The student wants to revise the draft to use words that help explain how ideas are connected. Read the draft of the report. Then complete the task that follows.

It's a good habit to work before playing. <u>When you get home from school, have a snack.</u> <u>Do your homework.</u> If your parents ask you to do some chores, do them right away after your homework. Finally, take some time to relax. You can play a game or watch TV. Just make sure you do your work before playing!

Choose the **best** word to connect the <u>underlined</u> sentences.

Ⓐ But

Ⓑ Finally,

Ⓒ Soon,

Ⓓ Then,

SESSION 2

Read the passage. Then answer the questions.

Arno's Neighbor

Arno's next-door neighbor is Mrs. Wills. She is 80 years old. Mrs. Wills lives alone, except for her dog Scooter. Arno likes to visit his neighbor. First, he takes Scooter for a walk. Mrs. Wills has trouble with her legs and cannot walk her dog. Arno likes walking Scooter because he does not have a dog of his own. Then he comes back and talks with Mrs. Wills for a while.

Mrs. Wills is an interesting person. She tells Arno stories about her childhood. It was very different from Arno's life. She and her family grew a lot of their own food in a garden. She lived in the country far from a town. She walked miles to get to school. Many of her toys were things her parents made for her. When she was really little, their house had no electricity!

She tells him about her favorite books. He tells her about his favorite books. Sometimes she recites funny poems for him. Arno likes this one:

In the Night

The night was growing old
As she trudged through snow and sleet;
Her nose was long and cold,
And her shoes were full of feet.

GO ON →

Mrs. Wills likes to hear about Arno's life. She asks what he is doing in school. She talks with him about baseball.

One spring day, Arno was thinking that he would like to do something nice for Mrs. Wills. When he got back from walking Scooter, Mrs. Wills was making her dinner. She opened a can of soup. Then she poured it into a pan to heat up. That gave Arno an idea.

When Arno got home, he told his mother and father about Mrs. Wills' soup and the garden she used to have.

"I bet she would really like some fresh vegetables and fruits this summer," said Arno.

"Do you have an idea?" Mom asked.

"My friend Lily's family rents a space in the city garden plot. They grow vegetables and fruits there. We could get a plot and grow food. We could use some, and we could give some to Mrs. Wills."

Arno's parents agreed. By June, Arno was picking berries, lettuce, and peas. Later in the summer, he gathered tomatoes, squash, and melons. Every day, he took some food to Mrs. Wills. She was excited about the treats he brought her.

Mrs. Wills got out some old recipes. She used to make these dishes for her family. Arno helped her make them. She kept some of the food for dinner and sent some home with Arno. Sometimes Arno's family went to Mrs. Wills' house, or she went to theirs. Then they enjoyed the delicious meals together.

GO ON →

One day, Arno and Mrs. Wills were making a big bowl of steaming vegetables with cheese on top. Mrs. Wills said, "You know, Arno, this was a very nice idea you had. You grow all this food and share it with me."

"But you have taught us all kinds of new recipes and ways to cook, too," said Arno. "We are helping each other!"

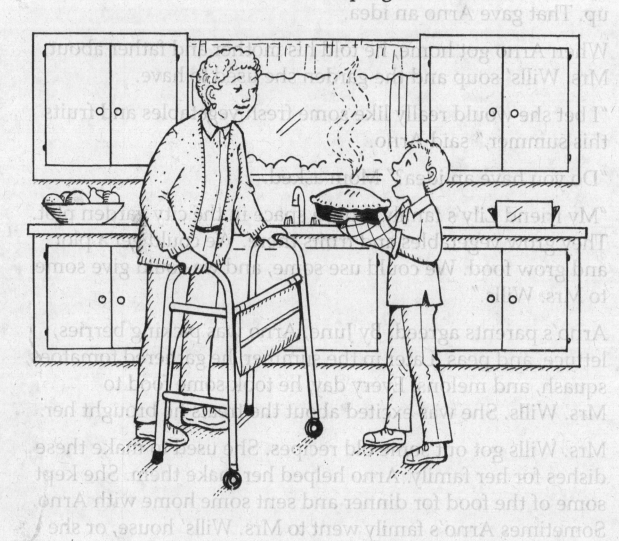

GO ON →

21 The following question has two parts. First, answer part A. Then, answer part B.

Part A: What conclusion can be drawn about Arno in paragraph 1 of the passage?

Ⓐ Arno helps Mrs. Wills.

Ⓑ Arno walks with Mrs. Wills.

Ⓒ Arno visits Mrs. Wills every day.

Ⓓ Arno wants Mrs. Wills to give him the dog.

Part B: Which sentence from paragraph 1 of the passage **best** helps you answer part A?

Ⓐ Arno's next-door neighbor is Mrs. Wills.

Ⓑ Arno likes to visit his neighbor.

Ⓒ First, he takes Scooter for a walk.

Ⓓ Then he comes back and talks with Mrs. Wills for a while.

22 The following question has two parts. First, answer part A. Then, answer part B.

Part A: Which sentence **best** tells the main message of the passage?

(A) Mrs. Wills and Arno need extra food.

(B) Mrs. Wills and Arno have an exciting life.

(C) Mrs. Wills and Arno share with each other.

(D) Mrs. Wills and Arno enjoy fruits and vegetables.

Part B: Which sentence from the passage **best** helps you answer part A?

(A) Mrs. Wills is an interesting person.

(B) "We could get a plot and grow food."

(C) Later in the summer, he gathered tomatoes, squash, and melons.

(D) Then they enjoyed the delicious meals together.

GO ON →

23 The following question has two parts. First, answer part A. Then, answer part B.

Part A: Read the sentences from the passage.

She tells him about her favorite books. He tells her about his favorite books. Sometimes she recites funny poems for him. Arno likes this one:

In the Night
The night was growing old
As she trudged through snow and sleet;
Her nose was long and cold,
And her shoes were full of feet.

Which of these **best** tells why the author **most likely** included a poem in the passage?

Ⓐ to show that Mrs. Wills likes to read

Ⓑ to explain that Mrs. Wills is an older woman

Ⓒ to tell the reader about what Mrs. Wills does at night

Ⓓ to let the reader know that Mrs. Wills has a good memory

Part B: Which sentence from the passage **best** helps you answer part A?

Ⓐ She is 80 years old.

Ⓑ She tells Arno stories about her childhood.

Ⓒ She lived in the country far from a town.

Ⓓ She tells him about her favorite books.

GO ON →

24 Read the poem from the passage.

The night was growing old
As she trudged through snow and sleet;
Her nose was long and cold,
And her shoes were full of feet.

Which of these could **best** replace the last line of the
poem and keep the same rhythm?

Ⓐ She had no heat.

Ⓑ And her home was down the street.

Ⓒ And there was a person she wanted to meet.

Ⓓ And her hair was the color of golden wheat.

GO ON →

25 The following question has two parts. First, answer part A. Then, answer part B.

Part A: What can the reader tell about Mrs. Wills from the passage?

Ⓐ She misses having a garden.

Ⓑ She knows that cooking takes time.

Ⓒ She likes eating canned soup in the evening.

Ⓓ She learns that helping friends is a lot of work.

Part B: Which sentence from the passage **best** helps you answer part A?

Ⓐ When he got back from walking Scooter, Mrs. Wills was making her dinner.

Ⓑ When Arno got home, he told his mother and father about Mrs. Wills' soup and the garden she used to have.

Ⓒ Mrs. Wills got out some old recipes.

Ⓓ She kept some of the food for dinner and sent some home with Arno.

26 Choose the words that **best** complete the sentence about the passage.

In the _____ of the story, once Arno gets home he _____.

(A) beginning, calls his friend

(B) beginning, cooks soup

(C) middle, talks to his parents

(D) end, plants a garden

27 Choose the words that **best** complete the sentences about the events in the passage.

Arno tells his parents that he wants to _____. After they hear what Arno has to say, Arno's parents _____.

(A) walk Mrs. Wills' dog, feel Arno is too young

(B) grow food for Mrs. Wills, like Arno's idea

(C) read stories to Mrs. Wills, help with Arno's garden

(D) make dinner for Mrs. Wills, think Arno will give up

GO ON →

28 Read the paragraphs from the passage. Then answer the question that follows.

One day, Arno and Mrs. Wills were making a big bowl of steaming vegetables with cheese on top. Mrs. Wills said, "You know, Arno, this was a very nice idea you had. You grow all this food and share it with me."

"But you have taught us all kinds of new recipes and ways to cook, too," said Arno. "We are helping each other!"

What is the main message that Arno learns? Use details from the passage in your answer.

_____

_____

_____

_____

_____

_____

Read the passage. Then answer the questions.

Bald Eagles

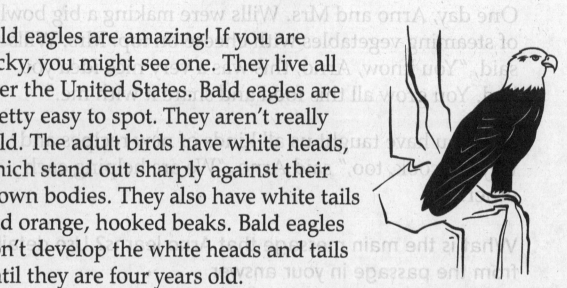

Bald eagles are amazing! If you are lucky, you might see one. They live all over the United States. Bald eagles are pretty easy to spot. They aren't really bald. The adult birds have white heads, which stand out sharply against their brown bodies. They also have white tails and orange, hooked beaks. Bald eagles don't develop the white heads and tails until they are four years old.

Bald eagles are big birds. They can weigh up to 14 pounds. They also have a large wingspan. That's the distance from the tip of one wing to the tip of the other. An eagle's wingspan can be as much as eight feet. Their strong, wide wings help them soar for hours.

Bald eagles have good eyesight. Their eyes are much sharper than human eyes. They use their eyes when they hunt. Bald eagles eat rodents, small mammals, and other small birds, but they mostly eat fish. Spotting a tasty fish dinner is easy for an eagle. Bald eagles can snatch fish right out of the water. Sometimes they even steal fish from other birds! They can dive as fast as 50 miles per hour. When an eagle catches a fish, it holds on tightly. Bald eagles have strong claws, called "talons," on their feet. Their talons are orange, like their beaks.

GO ON →

These birds are beautiful and strong. But they are threatened in some places. Much of their habitat has been destroyed. People cut down trees where they built nests. In the past, people also used to hunt bald eagles. And many bald eagles were hurt by a chemical called DDT. For many years, farmers used DDT to kill bugs.

Now there are laws to keep eagles safe. Today, DDT isn't used anymore. It is also illegal to hunt bald eagles. The number of bald eagles is growing. Healthy bald eagles can live for up to 30 years. Eagles that pair up stay together for life. They can have many babies. Bald eagles use sticks to build huge nests high in trees. The nests can measure up to eight feet across. They can weigh almost a ton. These strong nests can withstand storms and last for a long time!

The bald eagle is a symbol of America. It was chosen for its strength, long life, and proud looks. The bald eagle can be seen on the great seal of the United States. It is also found on quarters, half dollars, and gold coins. Many states also have bald eagles on their flags. It is one of the most loved symbols of our country.

GO ON →

29 The following question has two parts. First, answer part A. Then, answer part B.

Part A: Which conclusion about the author's purpose is supported by the passage?

- Ⓐ The author wanted to teach about the biggest birds in the world.

- Ⓑ The author wanted to teach about bald eagles.

- Ⓒ The author wanted to teach about how bald eagles hunt.

- Ⓓ The author wanted to teach about birds that like to eat fish.

Part B: Which sentence from the passage **best** supports your answer in part A?

- Ⓐ Bald eagles are amazing!

- Ⓑ They can weigh up to 14 pounds.

- Ⓒ They use their eyes when they hunt.

- Ⓓ Spotting a tasty fish dinner is easy for an eagle.

30 The following question has two parts. First, answer part A. Then, answer part B.

Part A: Read the sentences from the passage.

Spotting a tasty fish dinner is easy for an eagle. Bald eagles can <u>snatch</u> fish right out of the water. Sometimes they even steal fish from other birds! They can dive as fast as 50 miles per hour. When an eagle catches a fish, it holds on tightly."

What does the word <u>snatch</u> **most likely** mean?

(A) grab

(B) follow

(C) hunt

(D) see

Part B: Which phrase from the passage **best** supports your answer in part A?

(A) Spotting a tasty fish is easy

(B) Sometimes they even steal fish

(C) dive as fast as 50 miles per hour

(D) catches a fish, it holds on tightly

31 The following question has two parts. First, answer part A. Then, answer part B.

Part A: Read the sentences from the passage.

These birds are beautiful and strong. But they are threatened in some places. Much of their habitat has been destroyed. People cut down trees where they built nests. In the past, people also used to hunt bald eagles. And many bald eagles were hurt by a chemical called DDT. For many years, farmers used DDT to kill bugs.

Now there are laws to keep eagles safe. Today, DDT isn't used anymore. It is also illegal to hunt bald eagles. The number of bald eagles is growing. Healthy bald eagles can live for up to 30 years. Eagles that pair up stay together for life.

What is **one** cause why eagles are being threatened?

(A) People have done things to hurt eagles.

(B) Eagles are not laying enough healthy eggs.

(C) Eagles cannot hunt well enough to find food.

(D) People have not passed laws to protect eagles.

Part B: Which sentence from the passage **best** helps you answer part A?

(A) These birds are beautiful and strong.

(B) People cut down trees where they built nests.

(C) Healthy bald eagles can live for up to 30 years.

(D) Eagles that pair up stay together for life.

GO ON →

32 Match each main idea to its supporting detail from the passage.

Eagles are big.	Bald eagles can snatch fish right out of the water.
Eagles are threatened.	They can weigh up to 14 pounds.
Eagles are good hunters.	Much of their habitat has been destroyed.
Eagles are a symbol of America.	The bald eagle can be seen on the great seal of the United States.

33 Read the sentences from the passage.

Bald eagles are pretty easy to spot. They aren't really bald. The adult birds have white heads, which stand out sharply against their brown bodies.

What does the word spot **most likely** mean as it is used in the passage?

(A) stain　　　(C) see

(B) dot　　　(D) touch

GO ON →

Read the directions. Then answer the questions.

34 Read the sentence and the question that follows.

The boy was small and ran to his mother when he saw her.

Which **two** sentences are correct ways to change the sentence?

Ⓐ The small boy saw his mother and ran to her.

Ⓑ The mother saw the small boy and ran to her.

Ⓒ The mother ran when she saw the small boy.

Ⓓ The boy was small and ran when he saw his mother.

Ⓔ The boy ran to hug his small mother when he saw her.

Ⓕ The small boy ran to hug his mother when he saw her.

35 Which **two** sentences are written correctly?

Ⓐ My older sister drove himself to the park.

Ⓑ She should sing yourself to sleep at night.

Ⓒ The tiny puppy sat on the step all by itself.

Ⓓ The children tried to bake the cake theirselves.

Ⓔ My birds like to look at themselves in the mirror.

Ⓕ The little boy was so happy he tied his shoes by myself.

36 Which word correctly completes the sentence?

The puppy ran _____ across the yard.

   (A) fast

   (B) fluffy

   (C) happy

   (D) quickly

37 A student is writing a report for her class about frogs. The writer wants to use a word that will make her meaning clear. Choose the word that **best** completes the sentence.

Frogs lay their eggs in water. The eggs _____ into baby tadpoles. They will look a lot like fish. As the tadpoles grow, they turn into frogs. The tadpoles must live in the water. After they turn into frogs, they can live on land or in water.

   (A) become

   (B) hatch

   (C) open

   (D) tear

GO ON →

38 A student is writing an opinion paper for his class about roller coasters. Read the draft of the paper. Then answer the question that follows.

Roller coasters are rides that can be found at parks and fairs. Some people are afraid to get on them. I think they are great! There are many different kinds of roller coasters. Some are wooden. Some go very fast. Some turn upside down. Riding them is <u>an out of this world</u> thing to do!

What is a clearer way to say the <u>underlined</u> phrase?

Ⓐ a very different

Ⓑ a very fun

Ⓒ a dangerous

Ⓓ a strange

GO ON →

39 A student is writing a report for his class about dinosaurs. Read the draft of the report and answer the question that follows.

Dinosaurs lived very long ago. All that is left of them now are bones. I think it would be <u>cool</u> to have a pet dinosaur. You could ride it to school. It could reach things on high shelves for you. No one would bother you if you had a dinosaur for a pet. A dinosaur would be the best pet ever.

The student has decided that the <u>underlined</u> word is not a clear or good choice for the report. Choose the word that **best** replaces the <u>underlined</u> word.

Ⓐ troubling

Ⓑ hard

Ⓒ exciting

Ⓓ wild

STOP

Narrative Performance Task

Task:

Your class has been learning about exercise. Now your class is going to create a website to share what they have learned. As part of your research, you have found the following two sources.

Source #1: "Exercise"

Source #2: "Ways to Get Exercise"

After you have reviewed these sources, you will answer some questions about them. Briefly look over the sources and the three questions that follow. Then, go back and review the sources carefully to find the information you will need to answer the questions and write a story.

In Part 2, you will write your story using information from the two sources.

Directions for Part 1

You will now look at the two sources. You can look at the sources as often as you like.

Research Questions:

After looking at the sources, use the rest of the time in Part 1 to answer three questions about them. Your answers to these questions will be scored. Also your answers will help you think about the information you have read, which should help you write your story. You may look at the sources when you think it would be helpful. You may also look at your notes.

GO ON →

Source #1: Exercise

Did you know that when you play, you are also exercising? There are many ways to get exercise, like running or hopping. When you exercise, you use your muscles, heart, and lungs. Exercise makes you healthy and strong. Exercise is both healthy and fun.

Exercise keeps you healthy. It helps to control your weight so that you are less likely to become overweight. Exercise helps you to keep a healthy weight. It also helps to keep your blood pressure low. It keeps you from getting certain diseases. When you exercise, you can lower your chance of getting diabetes.

One way to exercise is to run. Running is good for your muscles, heart, and lungs. Your heart and lungs work faster when you run. Have a race with your friends. Play tag with your friends. Then, put your hand on your chest. Feel your heart beating, fast. Your heart works harder. Your lungs are working, too. You use your lungs to breathe while your heart pumps blood. Running is also a great way to make your bones stronger.

Just tying your shoe is also a way to exercise. Your heart does not beat faster. You do not breathe harder. But, when you bend down to tie your shoes, you do increase your flexibility. You are able to move your muscles more easily.

You should try to exercise for about 60 minutes every day. At school, you can exercise at recess or gym class. At home, you can go outside and play tag or jump rope. Playing kickball is also a way to get more exercise. Sometimes you may not be able to go outside. Then, you can exercise inside. You can help clean up your room. Or, you can dance to your favorite song.

GO ON →

Water is very important when you exercise. A way to exercise and stay strong is to be sure to drink plenty of water. Drink enough water to keep you from getting too thirsty. Not drinking enough water can make you feel sick or dizzy. When you exercise, drink plenty of water before you start an activity. Try to drink water about every 20 minutes while you exercise. Drink water when you finish to help you cool off.

Sometimes you can exercise too much or when it is too hot. If you start to feel bad, take a break and relax. Sit where it is cool or go inside. Continue to drink water. Certain times of the day are better to exercise than others. The best time to play is early in the morning or late afternoon when the weather is cool.

So, don't spend your day playing video games! Exercise is good for you and makes you feel good, too.

GO ON →

Source #2: Ways to Get Exercise

Have you ever played on the monkey bars, swings, or with a friend? When you play outside, you are exercising. There are many ways to exercise outside.

Playing on the monkey bars helps you stay fit. It also makes you stronger. First, jump up and reach for a bar with your hands. Once you reach it, hold on. Reach for the next bar in front with one hand. Don't let go! Then, reach with your other hand and keep going until you get to the end of the monkey bars.

Did you know that stretching and standing up straight is another way to exercise and have fun? It is also good for your muscles because it makes your muscles stronger. You can push against a tree or a wall. It makes your leg muscles strong. When you push a friend on the swings, you are stretching your arms and back muscles. You are making them stronger. When you are sitting on the swing, push your legs back and forth. You are stretching your leg muscles and making them stronger, too.

You can also play on the see-saw. The see-saw stretches your legs. You will need a partner. Sit on one end of the see-saw and your friend will sit on the other end. Then, one of you will go down and the other up. When you go down and your feet touch the ground, bend your knees and push back up. When you friend goes down, he will do the same.

Lots of kids play tag on the playground. You can chase your friends when playing tag. Or, a friend can chase you. Either way, you are running. When you run you make your heart beat faster. You breathe harder.

Whether playing on the monkey bars and swings, or chasing friends, exercise helps you stay healthy while having fun.

GO ON →

Name: _____ Date: _____

1 Draw a line from each source to the ideas that it supports.

	It is best to drink water before, during, and after exercising.
"Exercise"	Exercising on playground equipment works different muscles.
"Ways to Get Exercise"	Resting, just like exercise, is good for your body.
	Stretching helps make your muscles stronger.

2 Both sources tell about exercise. What does "Exercise" say about exercise that "Ways to Get Exercise" does not? Explain why that information is helpful for the reader. Give **two** details from "Exercise" to support your answer.

_____

_____

_____

_____

_____

_____

GO ON →

3 Each source talks about exercise. Why is this topic important? Use at least **one** example from "Exercise" and at least **one** example from "Ways to Get Exercise" to support your answer. For each example, include the source title or number.

_____

_____

_____

_____

_____

_____

Directions for Part 2

You will now look at your sources, take notes, and plan, write, revise, and edit your story. First read your assignment and the information about how your story will be scored. Then begin your work.

Your Assignment:

Now that you have learned about exercise, it is time to work on the website your class is making about Field Day. Field Day is an all-day, school event filled with sports and fun.

Your teacher has asked you to write a story about a student who is participating in Field Day. Write a story that is at least three paragraphs long about something that happens to the character during Field Day. Be sure to use the information that you learned from the sources when you write about your character.

Make sure your story includes a setting, gives information about the characters, and tells what happens. Remember to use words that describe and don't just tell. Your story should have a clear beginning, middle, and end.

REMEMBER: A well-written story

- has a clear plot and clear sequence of events
- is well-organized and has a point of view
- uses details from the sources to support your story
- uses clear language
- follows rules of writing (spelling, punctuation, and grammar)

Now begin work on your story. Manage your time carefully so that you can plan, write, revise, and edit your story. Write your response on a separate sheet of paper.

Informational Performance Task

Task:
Your class has been learning about seasons. Now your class is going to create a class project to share what you have learned. As part of your research, you have found the following two sources.

Source #1: "Seasons"

Source #2: "Seasons in the Arctic and Antarctic"

After you have reviewed these sources, you will answer some questions about them. Briefly look over the sources and the three questions that follow. Then, go back and review the sources carefully to find the information you will need to answer the questions and write an informational article.

In Part 2, you will write your article using information from the two sources.

Directions for Part 1
You will now look at the two sources. You can look at the sources as often as you like.

Research Questions:
After looking at the sources, use the rest of the time in Part 1 to answer three questions about them. Your answers to these questions will be scored. Also your answers will help you think about the information you have read, which should help you write your article. You may look at the sources when you think it would be helpful. You may also look at your notes.

GO ON →

Source #1: Seasons

You do not need a calendar to know when it is fall. In the northern parts of the United States, fall brings many changes. The leaves turn colors. Some are red, some yellow, and some orange. They fall from the trees. They cover the grass and sidewalks. They make swishing sounds when people step on them. Children love this!

Many fall days are cool, but some days are still warm and sunny. Even hot days end with cool nights. Some nights are really cold! In the morning, you can see white frost on the grass.

Animals and birds get ready for winter. You can see squirrels looking for food. They look very busy! You can see lots of geese. Big flocks of these birds fly overhead. They band together to fly south. They stay there through the cold winter.

Winter comes after fall. It brings long, dark nights. In the winter, it is cold outside. Everything is frozen. Some animals sleep to stay warm. They sleep all day and all night. Bears sleep in their cozy dens, and squirrels are safe in their trees.

Winter also brings snow! Families go sledding on slippery hills, and children build snowmen. Ice covers bare tree branches. It sparkles when the sun comes out. But even when it's sunny, it's still cold!

Finally, the snow starts to melt. Days are longer and nights are shorter. The weather warms, and green grass appears. Spring arrives after winter. It is when everything grows again. Trees bloom with pink and white flowers. Tulips poke their colorful heads above the ground.

GO ON →

Birds flutter to and fro, building nests and laying eggs. Bears wake up and come out from their dens. They blink and stretch in the warm sunlight. Squirrels run up and down their trees again. Geese fill the skies as they return from their winter in the south. Children rush outside to play in the soft grass and plant gardens. They press seeds deep into the warm dirt.

Soon, the days grow longer. The sun is bright and hot. Summer is here! The trees grow thick with green leaves. Baby birds hatch from eggs, and sing songs from their nests. Bear cubs play in the forest. They tumble and roll down hills. They hunt for and eat ripe berries. Families picnic outside. They go on vacations. They travel to the lake or beach and play in the sand. Children build sandcastles and swim in the cool water. They go to the park and play ball. Summer is a fun time to be outdoors!

Soon, the weather will change. The days will get shorter. The nights will get cooler and longer. The animals and birds will get ready for winter. The leaves on the trees will slowly change from green to gold. Then, it will be fall again!

Copyright © McGraw-Hill Education

GO ON →

GO ON →

Source #2: Seasons in the Arctic and Antarctic

The reason we have seasons is because Earth is tilted. It stays tilted as it moves around the sun. Most of the people on Earth live near the middle of the planet. There, it is not so tilted. The sun's rays come almost straight down. There, the hours of daylight and darkness are about the same. The seasons change about every three months: the four seasons of fall, winter, spring and summer.

However, there are places on Earth that are not near the middle. They do not experience four seasons; they experience two: winter and summer. One such place is called the Arctic. It is mostly water with land all around it. The Arctic is near the North Pole. Another is called the Antarctic. Unlike the Arctic, it is mostly land with water around it. The Antarctic is near the South Pole.

For six months, the Arctic is tilted away from the sun. This is the winter season. It is cold and dark. It snows a lot, and the ice never melts. Many days, it is dark all day and night! People try to stay inside. But, they still have to go to work. Children have to go to school. They turn on lots of lights! The dark days last from October through December. Then, the sunlight slowly returns. As winter turns to summer, the days get longer and longer.

Finally, summer comes. Some of the ice starts to thaw in May. The Arctic is now tilted towards the sun for six months. Much of the snow melts. Then, it is sunny all day and night! All summer, the sun stays up. It is light all day long. It is light at night! This is why the Arctic is called "The Land of the Midnight Sun." People put dark curtains on their windows so they can sleep. But it can be hard to sleep when the sun is out! So, sometimes they don't sleep. Sometimes they play baseball games in the middle of the night instead!

GO ON →

Since the Antarctic has far less water than the Arctic, it is much colder. Like the Arctic, the Antarctic also only has two seasons. But the seasons are during different months. When the Arctic is tilted toward the sun, the Antarctic is tilted away from it. So when it is winter in the Arctic, it is summer in the Antarctic. When it is summer in the Arctic, it is winter in the Antarctic.

Unlike the Arctic, there are no towns in the Antarctic. People can't live there very easily. A few scientists live on small bases on the ice. They study the ice and animals. In the winter, around 10 people live on bases. In the summer, the number might be closer to 50. But even in the summer, the ice does not melt. It is still very cold! Still, at least it is light. When it is light, it is easier for the scientists to work.

GO ON →

1 Choose **two** details below that explain what **both** "Seasons" and "Seasons in the Arctic and Antarctic" say about winter.

Ⓐ It is sunny all day long.

Ⓑ It brings long, dark nights.

Ⓒ It is when everything grows again.

Ⓓ It snows a lot, and the ice never melts.

Ⓔ It is when the Earth stays tilted as it moves around the sun.

2 Both sources tell about seasons. Explain what you have learned about seasons. Use **one** detail from **each** source to support your explanation. For each detail, include the source title or number.

_____

_____

_____

_____

_____

_____

3 Explain why people spend more time outside in the summer than in the winter. Give **two** reasons, **one** from "Seasons" and **one** from "Seasons in the Arctic and Antarctic." For each reason, include the source title or number.

_____

_____

_____

GO ON →

Directions for Part 2

You will now look at your sources, take notes, and plan, write, revise, and edit your article. First read your assignment and the information about how your article will be scored. Then begin your work.

Your Assignment:

Your class has been learning about seasons in different parts of the world. Your teacher has asked you to write an informational article comparing seasons in the northern parts of the United States to seasons in the Arctic and Antarctic.

Using more than one source, develop a main idea. Choose the most important information from the sources to support your main idea. Then, write an informational article that is at least three paragraphs long. Clearly organize your article and support your main idea with details from the sources.

Use your own words except when quoting directly from the sources. Be sure to give the source title or number when using details from the sources.

REMEMBER: A well-written informational article

- has a clear main idea
- is well-organized and stays on the topic
- has an introduction, a conclusion, and transitions
- uses details from the sources to support your main idea
- follows rules of writing (spelling, punctuation, and grammar)

Now begin work on your informational article. Manage your time carefully so that you can plan, write, revise, and edit your informational article. Write your response on a separate sheet of paper.

Opinion Performance Task

Task:
Your class has been learning about Earth Day. Now you are going to write an opinion article. As part of your research you have found the following two sources.

Source #1: "Earth Day"

Source #2: "Ways to Celebrate Earth Day"

After you have reviewed these sources, you will answer some questions about them. Briefly look over the sources and the three questions that follow. Then, go back and review the sources carefully to find the information you will need to answer the questions and write an opinion article.

In Part 2, you will write your article using information from the two sources.

Directions for Part 1
You will now look at the two sources. You can look at any of the sources as often as you like.

Research Questions:
After looking at the sources, use the rest of the time in Part 1 to answer three questions about them. Your answers to these questions will be scored. Also your answers will help you think about the information you have read, which should help you write your article. You may refer to the sources when you think it would be helpful. You may also look at your notes.

GO ON →

Source #1: Earth Day

America has all kinds of holidays. Holidays are special days that people celebrate. Some are to honor people. Some holidays help us remember the past. One special day reminds us to think about our Earth. This day is called Earth Day.

In the 1960s, Earth was filled with pollution. Pollution happens when the environment is made dirty. This can happen when people do not correctly get rid of garbage, chemicals, or other harmful things. People did not think very much about the damage that cars and trash did to Earth. Many people did not know how to take care of the land, water, and air. They did not know how important it was to keep Earth clean. In 1969, a group of leaders met to talk about the environment. They decided to make a special day to celebrate our planet.

The first Earth Day was held on April 22 of 1970. Newspapers and other media told the people about Earth Day. Many people were excited about the holiday. They wanted to participate. Over 20 million people in America joined to celebrate taking care of our Earth. There were events all across the country. Cities and towns held fairs. Schools and colleges took part, too. The day was a teaching day. People learned that we should take better care of Earth. They thought of ideas that would help. They talked about stopping water, air, and land pollution. They talked about ways to take care of resources and save the planet. Resources we need from our Earth are air, water, and soil. They learned these resources need to stay clean so we can use them.

GO ON →

The first Earth Day was a big success. It made people think about the environment. It helped bring about new groups and laws. The U.S. Environmental Protection Agency and the Clean Air Act were made. More people wanted to celebrate Earth. They wanted to learn how to keep it clean.

Other countries began to celebrate Earth Day, too. Now over 180 countries celebrate Earth Day. Over 5,000 groups all across the world take part in activities. They help to tell people about saving and taking care of Earth. An Earth Day flag was even made. The flag is dark blue and has a real picture of Earth on it. The picture was taken from space by NASA.

We celebrate Earth Day every spring. It helps us remember that Earth still needs our care. We need to take care of the resources Earth gives us. We need to stop pollution. Earth Day teaches us there are many ways that people can celebrate our world and help protect it.

GO ON →

Source #2: Ways to Celebrate Earth Day

Many people know that it is important to save our Earth. They know that they should not pollute the land, air, and water. They know trash is bad for the environment. They understand that Earth Day is a special day to remember the planet. However, some people may not know how many different ways there are to celebrate Earth Day.

Planting trees and flowers is a good way to celebrate Earth Day. The plants make Earth look pretty. The roots of the plants help the soil. They hold plants in place and prevent erosion. Erosion is when water or wind wash or blow away the soil. Plants also help the animals. They give animals food and shelter.

Recycling is a great way to help Earth. Collect paper, plastics, and metals. Put them in recycling bins. Recycling companies will collect the materials. They turn them into new products for people to use. Groups of people can have recycling contests to encourage more people to help. Ask schools, clubs, and churches to help.

Upcycling is a fun and exciting way to celebrate Earth Day. Upcycling is taking used materials and making them into something that can be used. Crafts and toy projects are fun to upcycle. Make birdhouses from milk cartons. Empty cardboard tubes can be turned into play telescopes and binoculars. Add jewels and designs to old clothing to upcycle them into new things to wear.

Conserving resources is a way that many people celebrate Earth Day. People conserve and protect resources. They are careful how they use them. Turning off lights when they are not being used conserves energy. Growing garden vegetables

GO ON →

and fruits is good for the soil. It also saves energy. Factories do not have to process food you eat from your garden. No one has to drive to the store to deliver or buy it. Air is protected by walking instead of driving cars that use fuel. Save water by turning it off when brushing your teeth. Quick showers use less water than filling bathtubs. Reusing shopping bags or containers is another way to conserve resources.

Teaching others about saving Earth is an important way to celebrate Earth Day. Teach friends and family about ways they can help. Remind them about conserving water, air, and energy. Do an upcycle project together. Show them recycle bins or hand out recycle bags for them to fill.

Clean-up events are a way to help Earth. It also makes a place look better. Organize a group of people to pick up trash at a park or school. Put trash in its place. When trash is put away correctly, it will not pollute the water, land, and air. Any trash that can be recycled should be placed in recycle bags and bins.

Earth Day is a great day for people to remember how important Earth is to us. There are many ways to help Earth by teaching others. Stopping pollution and conserving resources help Earth. It is important to celebrate Earth Day. It is also important to remember that Earth needs to be protected every day.

GO ON →

1 Choose **two** details below that explain what **both** "Earth Day" and "Ways to Celebrate Earth Day" say about how to save Earth.

Ⓐ Planting trees and flowers is a good way to celebrate Earth Day.

Ⓑ Recycling is a great way to help Earth.

Ⓒ Upcycling is a fun and exciting way to celebrate Earth Day.

Ⓓ Conserving resources is a way that many people celebrate Earth Day.

Ⓔ Quick showers use less water than filling bathtubs.

Ⓕ When trash is put away correctly, it will not pollute the water, land, and air.

2 "Earth Day" tells about Earth Day. Explain how the information in "Ways to Celebrate Earth Day" helps the reader understand Earth Day. Give **two** details from "Ways to Celebrate Earth Day" to support your explanation.

_____

_____

_____

_____

3 Which source do you think has the **most helpful** information for understanding how to care for Earth? Explain why you think this source is the **most helpful**. Support your explanation with **two** details from the source. For each detail, include the source title or number.

_____

_____

_____

_____

_____

_____

GO ON →

Directions for Part 2

You will now look at your sources, take notes, and plan, write, revise, and edit your article. First read your assignment and the information about how your article will be scored. Then begin your work.

Your Assignment:

Your school uses a lot of paper and plastic materials. Many people think that recycling is a better way to get rid of these materials. These people want students to put recyclable materials in recycling bins.

Your teacher has asked you to write an opinion article about the problem to share with the principal. Your assignment is to use the information from sources to write an opinion article in which you agree or disagree with having a recycling project at school. Make sure you clearly state your opinion and write two to three paragraphs supporting your opinion with reasons and details from the sources.

Explain your ideas clearly and use your own words, except when quoting directly from the sources. Be sure to give the source title or number for the details or facts you use.

REMEMBER: A well-written opinion article

- has a clear opinion
- is well-organized and stays on the topic
- has an introduction, a conclusion, and transitions
- uses facts from the sources to support your opinion
- follows rules of writing (spelling, punctuation, and grammar)

Now begin work on your opinion article. Manage your time carefully so that you can plan, write, revise, and edit your opinion article. Write your response on a separate sheet of paper.

Answer Key

Name: _____

Question	Correct Answer	Content Focus	CCSS	Complexity
1	B	Multiple-Meaning Words	L.2.4a	DOK 1
2A	C	Plot: Problem and Solution	RL.2.5	DOK 2
2B	D	Plot: Problem and Solution/Text Evidence	RL.2.5/RL.2.1	DOK 2
3	A	Root Words	L.2.4c	DOK 1
4	see below	Character, Setting, Plot	RL.2.3	DOK 2
5	see below	Character, Setting, Plot	RL.2.3	DOK 3
6A	B	Author's Purpose	RI.2.6	DOK 2
6B	C	Author's Purpose/Text Evidence	RI.2.6/RI.2.1	DOK 2
7A	D	Author's Purpose	RI.2.8	DOK 2
7B	B	Author's Purpose/Text Evidence	RI.2.8/RI.2.1	DOK 2
8A	D	Main Idea and Key Details	RI.2.1	DOK 2
8B	C	Main Idea and Key Details/Text Evidence	RI.2.1	DOK 2
9A	A	Context Clues: Sentence Clues	L.2.4a	DOK 2
9B	D	Context Clues: Sentence Clues/Text Evidence	L.2.4a/RI.2.1	DOK 2
10A	A	Author's Purpose	RI.2.8	DOK 2
10B	B	Author's Purpose/Text Evidence	RI.2.8/RI.2.1	DOK 2
11	B, E, F	Main Idea and Key Details	RI.2.1	DOK 2
12	D	Compound Words	L.2.4d	DOK 1
13	A	Author's Purpose	RI.2.6	DOK 3
14	C, E	Research	W.2.8	DOK 2
15	see below	Research	W.2.8	DOK 2
16	C	Research	W.2.8	DOK 2
17	D	Research	W.2.8	DOK 2

Question	Correct Answer	Content Focus	CCSS	Complexity
BENCHMARK ASSESSMENT — TEST 1				
18	see below	Opinion: Drafting, Editing, Revising	W.2.1	DOK 3
19	D	Informational: Drafting, Editing, Revising	W.2.2	DOK 2
20	A	Narrative: Drafting, Editing, Revising	W.2.3	DOK 2
21A	D	Plot: Problem and Solution	RL.2.5	DOK 2
21B	B	Plot: Problem and Solution/ Text Evidence	RL.2.5/RL.2.1	DOK 2
22A	B	Plot: Sequence	RL.2.5	DOK 2
22B	C	Plot: Sequence/Text Evidence	RL.2.5/RL.2.1	DOK 2
23A	C	Character, Setting, Plot	RL.2.3	DOK 2
23B	D	Character, Setting, Plot/Text Evidence	RL.2.3/RL.2.1	DOK 2
24	see below	Plot: Sequence	RL.2.5	DOK 2
25	D, E	Compound Words	L.2.4d	DOK 2
26	D	Character, Setting, Plot	RL.2.3	DOK 2
27	B	Context Clues: Sentence Clues	L.2.4a	DOK 2
28	see below	Plot: Problem and Solution	RL.2.5	DOK 3
29A	C	Author's Purpose	RI.2.8	DOK 2
29B	B	Author's Purpose/Text Evidence	RI.2.8/RI.2.1	DOK 2
30A	C	Context Clues: Sentence Clues	L.2.4a	DOK 2
30B	B	Context Clues: Sentence Clues/ Text Evidence	L.2.4a/RI.2.1	DOK 2
31A	C	Simile	L.2.5a	DOK 2
31B	D	Simile/Text Evidence	L.2.5a/RI.2.1	DOK 2
32	A, F	Main Idea and Key Details	RI.2.2	DOK 2
33	A	Author's Purpose	RI.2.6	DOK 2
34	B, D	Collective Nouns	L.2.1a	DOK 2

BENCHMARK ASSESSMENT — TEST 1

Question	Correct Answer	Content Focus	CCSS	Complexity
35	C, E	Past-Tense Verbs	L.2.1d	DOK 2
36	A	Singular and Plural Nouns	L.2.1b	DOK 2
37	A	Revising	W.2.3	DOK 2
38	C	Revising	W.2.1	DOK 2
39	B	Revising	W.2.3	DOK 2

Comprehension: Selected Response 2A, 2B, 4, 6A, 6B, 7A, 7B, 9A, 9B, 10A, 10B, 11, 13, 21A, 21B, 22A, 22B, 23A, 23B, 24, 26, 29A, 29B, 32, 33	/32	%
Comprehension: Constructed Response 5, 28	/4	%
Vocabulary 1, 3, 8A, 8B, 12, 25, 27, 30A, 30B, 31A, 31B	/16	%
Research 14, 15, 16, 17	/8	%
Drafting, Editing, Revising 18, 19, 20, 37, 38, 39	/12	%
English Language Conventions 34, 35, 36	/6	%
Total Benchmark Assessment Score	/78	%

4   Students should match the following characters and events as follows: Crow: recites a poem. Owl: explains what happened. Mouse: is friendly to Duck. Duck: helps Cricket. Rabbit: gives acorns to Squirrel.

5   **2-point response:** At first the animals argue a lot and are very selfish. Crow tries different ways to make them change, but they do not listen to him. Then Rabbit tells Squirrel about some acorns. Next, Squirrel gives Mouse some twigs for her nest. Soon all the animals start to act in a kind and helpful way.

15   Students should match the following main ideas and notes as follows:
• Main Idea: How Big Do Butterflies Grow; Note: Queen Alexandra's Birdwing is the largest butterfly.
• Main Idea: What Butterflies Look Like; Notes: Butterflies have four wings. Tiny scales on butterflies make them colorful.
• Main Idea: What Butterflies Eat; Note: Butterflies can suck nectar from flowers.

18   **2-point response:** Frozen yogurt has less sugar than ice cream. Students will have more desserts to choose from during lunchtime. We can choose ice cream sometimes. But, if we want a healthier choice, we can choose frozen yogurt. Serving frozen yogurt will help kids eat less sugar. I hope you will think about selling frozen yogurt.

Name: _____

24 Students should order the events as follows: 1. Aunt Becky gave him special clothes to put on. 2. She took him into the surgery room. 3. Jack looked at the tiny dog on the table. 4. Before he knew it, she was done.

28 **2-point response:** Aunt Becky wants Jack to learn about her job on Bring a Child to Work Day. Jack is worried about what he will see at the animal hospital, but he does not want to hurt her feelings. He goes with her to the animal hospital, and she shows him how she helps sick animals. By the end of the story, Jack changes his mind about Aunt Becky's job. He thinks he might be a vet someday, too.

104   Grade 2 • Benchmark Assessment

Question	Correct Answer	Content Focus	CCSS	Complexity
1A	D	Theme	RL.2.2	DOK 2
1B	C	Theme/Text Evidence	RL.2.2/ RL.2.1	DOK 2
2	B	Synonyms	L.4.5c	DOK 1
3A	D	Theme	RL.2.2	DOK 2
3B	A	Theme/Text Evidence	RL.2.2/ RL.2.1	DOK 2
4	D	Plot: Compare and Contrast	RL.2.5	DOK 2
5	see below	Character, Setting, Plot	RL.2.3	DOK 3
6A	A	Connections Within Text: Cause and Effect	RI.2.5	DOK 2
6B	B	Connections Within Text: Cause and Effect/Text Evidence	RI.2.5/RI.2.1	DOK 2
7A	B	Context Clues: Paragraph Clues	L.2.4a	DOK 2
7B	A	Context Clues: Paragraph Clues/Text Evidence	L.2.4a/RI.2.1	DOK 2
8	C	Idioms	L.4.5b	DOK 2
9A	C	Author's Purpose	RI.2.6	DOK 2
9B	A	Author's Purpose/Text Evidence	RI.2.6/RI.2.1	DOK 2
10A	B	Author's Purpose	RI.2.8	DOK 2
10B	C	Author's Purpose/Text Evidence	RI.2.8/RI.2.1	DOK 2
11	A, B	Connections Within Text: Cause and Effect	RI.2.3	DOK 3
12	see below	Connections Within Text: Sequence	RI.2.3	DOK 3
13	A	Main Idea and Details	RI.2.2	DOK 2
14	A, C	Research	W.2.8	DOK 2
15	E, F	Research	W.2.8	DOK 2
16	C	Research	W.2.8	DOK 2
17	C	Research	W.2.8	DOK 2

BENCHMARK ASSESSMENT — TEST 2

Question	Correct Answer	Content Focus	CCSS	Complexity
BENCHMARK ASSESSMENT — TEST 2				
18	see below	Narrative: Drafting, Editing, Revising	W.2.3	DOK 3
19	D	Opinion: Drafting, Editing, Revising	W.2.1	DOK 2
20	D	Informational: Drafting, Editing, Revising	W.2.3	DOK 2
21A	A	Character, Setting, Plot	RL.2.3	DOK 2
21B	B	Character, Setting, Plot/Text Evidence	RL.2.3/RL.2.1	DOK 2
22A	C	Theme	RL.2.2	DOK 3
22B	D	Theme/Text Evidence	RL.2.2/ RL.2.1	DOK 3
23A	A	Key Details	RL.2.1	DOK 2
23B	D	Key Details/Text Evidence	RL.2.1	DOK 2
24	B	Rhythm	RL.2.4	DOK 2
25A	A	Character, Setting, Plot	RL.2.3	DOK 2
25B	B	Character, Setting, Plot/Text Evidence	RL.2.3/RL.2.1	DOK 2
26	C	Plot: Sequence	RL.2.5	DOK 2
27	B	Plot: Sequence	RL.2.5	DOK 2
28	see below	Theme	RL.2.2	DOK 3
29A	B	Author's Purpose	RI.2.6	DOK 2
29B	A	Author's Purpose/Text Evidence	RI.2.6/RI.2.1	DOK 2
30A	A	Context Clues: Paragraph Clues	L.2.4a	DOK 2
30B	D	Context Clues: Paragraph Clues/Text Evidence	L.2.4a/RI.2.1	DOK 2
31A	A	Connections Within Text: Cause and Effect	RI.2.3	DOK 2
31B	B	Connections Within Text: Cause and Effect/Text Evidence	RI.2.3/RI.2.1	DOK 2
32	see below	Main Idea and Key Details	RI.2.2	DOK 2

BENCHMARK ASSESSMENT — TEST 2

Question	Correct Answer	Content Focus	CCSS	Complexity
33	C	Multiple-Meaning Words	L.2.4a	DOK 2
34	A, F	Combining and Rearranging Sentences	L.2.1f	DOK 2
35	C, E	Pronouns and Antecedents	L.2.1.c	DOK 2
36	D	Adjectives and Adverbs	L.2.1.e	DOK 2
37	B	Revising	W.2.2	DOK 2
38	B	Revising	W.2.1	DOK 2
39	C	Revising	W.2.2	DOK 2

Comprehension: Selected Response 1A, 1B, 3A, 3B, 4, 6A, 6B, 9A, 9B, 10A, 10B, 11, 12, 13, 21A, 21B, 22A, 22B, 23A, 23B, 24, 25A, 25B, 26, 27, 29A, 29B, 31A, 31B, 32	/38	%
Comprehension: Constructed Response 5, 28	/4	%
Vocabulary 2, 7A, 7B, 8, 30A, 30B, 33	/10	%
Research 14, 15, 16, 17	/8	%
Drafting, Editing, Revising 18, 19, 20, 37, 38, 39	/12	%
English Language Conventions 34, 35, 36	/6	%
Total Benchmark Assessment Score	/78	%

5. **2-point response:** Lang liked the celebration. She liked that everyone shared different foods and customs from their home countries. She was thankful for her new friends.

12. Students should order the events as follows: 1. The plant heats itself. 2. The plant's smell spreads. 3. Insects come to the plant. 4. Insects get pollen on their feet. 5. Insects carry pollen to other plants.

18. **2-point response:** First one team scored. Then the other team scored. In the ninth inning, the batter hit a home run. Dale didn't catch the ball, but he was still happy. The home team won! Dale talked about the game all the way home. He couldn't wait to go to another baseball game!

28 **2-point response:** Although Mrs. Wills is older, Arno learns many things from her. They learn by helping each other. He learns new recipes and new ways to cook. Arno learns about Mrs. Wills' life when she was a child. He learns how to cook the vegetables and fruits that are grown in the garden.

32 Students should match the following main ideas and details as follows:
- Main Idea: Eagles are big. Detail: They can weigh up to 14 pounds.
- Main Idea: Eagles are threatened. Detail: Much of their habitat has been destroyed.
- Main Idea: Eagles are good hunters. Detail: Bald eagles can snatch fish right out of the water.
- Main Idea: Eagles are a symbol of America. Detail: The bald eagle can be seen on the great seal of the United States.

Answer Key

		Narrative Performance Task		
Question	**Answer**	**CCSS**	**Complexity**	**Score**
1	see below	RI.2.1, RI.2.2, RI.2.3, RI.2.8, RI.2.9 W.2.2, W.2.3, W.2.8 L.2.1, L.2.2	DOK 3	/1
2	see below		DOK 3	/2
3	see below		DOK 3	/2
Story	see below		DOK 4	/4 [P/O] /4 [D/E] /2 [C]
Total Score				**/15**

1 Students should match each source with two ideas as follows:

"Exercise": Resting, just like exercise, is good for your body./ It is best to drink water before, during, and after exercising.
"Ways to Get Exercise": Exercising on playground equipment works different muscles./ Stretching helps make your muscles stronger.

2 **2-point response:** "Exercise" tells how to keep from getting sick when you exercise. "Ways to Get Exercise" tells about exercise but does not talk about ways to keep from getting sick. You should drink lots of water and exercise when it is cool. "Exercise" says to drink water about every 20 minutes. "Exercise" also says that if you drink water you will not get dizzy or sick. It also says to exercise when it is cool outside, such as early in the morning or late afternoon. This information is important because it helps to keep your body healthy.

3 **2-point response:** Source #1 says exercise keeps you fit and strong. Running keeps your heart and lungs strong. You stay flexible when tying your shoe. Source #2 says playing on monkey bars, swings, and see-saws makes your muscles strong. Source #1 talks about how much exercise to get. Do not exercise too much. Be safe by drinking lots of water and exercising when it is cool outside. Source #2 tells how to play on equipment. That way, if I don't know how to use the equipment I can still exercise because I have some directions.

10-point anchor paper: Kim tied her shoelaces and walked outside to the big field. Today was her school's Field Day. Kim was excited, but also knew that exercising helps to keep her healthy. Kim drank water from her water bottle—that was important.

"Oh-no!" Kim yelled. Her shoelace was untied. She bent down to tie it. Kim knows that tying her shoe makes her able to move easily. She is flexible. Then Kim stretched her arms and legs. She decided to push against the wall to make her legs stronger. Then she saw her friend Violet on the swings. "Violet, do you mind if I push you a little?" Kim questioned. "No, go ahead," said Violet. So Kim pushed Violet. It helped to make Kim's back muscles strong. But it also helped Violet. When Violet swung her legs on the swing, her leg muscles stretched.

It was finally time for Field Day to begin. Kim ran in a race against her classmates. She won second place! After the race, her heart was beating so fast, pumping blood through her body. She breathed harder, too. Running made her heart and lungs stronger.

Kim knew that after the race she needed to drink a bit more water, but she could not find her water bottle. "There you are!" shouted Violet. "You left your water bottle by the swings. I thought you might need it," said Violet. Kim was so glad that Violet had found her water bottle. Kim knew that after running, she would need water so she wouldn't feel dizzy.

Name: _____

Informational Performance Task				
Question	Answer	CCSS	Complexity	Score
1	B, D		DOK 3	/1
2	see below	RI.2.1, RI.2.2, RI.2.3, RI.2.8, RI.2.9 W.2.2, W.2.8 L.2.1, L.2.2	DOK 3	/2
3	see below		DOK 3	/2
Informational Article	see below		DOK 4	/4 [P/O] /4 [E/E] /2 [C]
Total Score				/15

2 **2-point response:** I learned that some places on Earth have four seasons, but some only have two seasons. In "Seasons," it says that the northern parts of the United States have four seasons: fall, winter, spring, and summer. In "Seasons in the Arctic and Antarctic," it says that the Arctic and Antarctic only have two seasons.

3 **2-point response:** "Seasons" says that people go on vacation outdoors during the summer because the sun is bright and hot. In "Seasons in the Arctic and Antarctic," it says that scientists study the outdoors during the summer because the days are longer and there is more light.

10-point anchor paper: You might have learned that there are four seasons, and this is true in a lot of places. But, it is not true in at least two places! Although the northern parts of the United States have four seasons, the Arctic and Antarctic only have two.

Summer in the northern U.S. is very different from summer in the Arctic and Antarctic. "Seasons" says that summers are bright and hot in the northern U.S. They are hot enough for children to plant gardens and go swimming. Summer in the Arctic and Antarctic are not nearly as hot. This is especially true in the Antarctic, where the ice never melts!

Winter in the northern U.S. can be cold and dark, but the sun still comes up during the day, even if it isn't bright. But according to "Seasons in the Arctic and Antarctic," winters there are dark day and night, for many weeks. People in the Arctic have to go to school and to their jobs in the dark!

I am not sure I would like such a long, dark winter. Although, it would be fun to have a long summer! The article "Seasons in the Arctic and Antarctic" states that people play baseball at night during the summer because it is light out all night! Still, I like having four seasons. I think I would rather live in the northern part of the U.S.!

Opinion Performance Task

Question	Answer	CCSS	Complexity	Score
1	D, F	RI.2.1, RI.2.2, RI.2.3, RI.2.8, RI.2.9 W.2.1, W.2.2, W.2.8 L.2.1, L.2.2	DOK 3	/1
2	see below		DOK 3	/2
3	see below		DOK 3	/2
Opinion Article	see below		DOK 4	/4 [P/O] /4 [E/E] /2 [C]
Total Score				/15

2 **2-point response:** "Earth Day" tells what Earth Day is and how it was started. "Ways to Celebrate Earth Day" adds to our understanding about Earth Day by giving examples of how people can celebrate Earth Day and take care of Earth. "Ways to Celebrate Earth Day" says recycling is a great way to help Earth. It tells how plastics and paper can be put into recycle bins. "Ways to Celebrate Earth Day" also tells that upcycling is a fun and exciting way to celebrate Earth Day. It talks about using old materials to make craft and toy projects.

3 **2-point response:** I think Source 2, "Ways to Celebrate Earth Day," has the most helpful information about caring for the Earth. It gives ideas and activities a reader can do in his or her home and community to help Earth. It says turning off lights when they are not being used conserves energy. Saving water by turning it off when brushing your teeth, taking quick showers use less water than filling bathtubs, and reusing shopping bags are ways to conserve resources. Source 2 has helpful information about how to care for Earth.

10-point anchor paper: Taking care of Earth and its resources is very important. Earth Day was started so people could learn more about taking care of Earth. In the two sources, we learn about Earth Day and ways to celebrate it. Source 2, "Ways to Celebrate Earth Day," tells the reader that recycling is one way to save Earth.

Beginning a recycling project at school is a good idea. Students should have to put recyclable materials in recycling bins. Recycling helps save Earth. Source 1, "Earth Day," tells us that pollution can happen when people do not get rid of garbage the right way. Recycling is the proper way to get rid of plastics and paper. When materials are recycled, they cannot become pollution. In Source 2, we learn that when items are placed into recycling bins, companies take the items. They change the old items into new items that people can use. Energy is conserved because new materials are not needed.

Students at school can help save Earth by placing paper and plastic materials into the recycling bins. When these materials are not placed into recycling bins, they become trash. Trash can pollute Earth. It makes Earth dirty. By beginning a recycling project at school, students can help keep Earth clean and healthy for people to live.